GRANNY WAS A SPY

GRANNY WAS A SPY

JOSE VILLIERS

Quartet Books
London · New York

First published by Quartet Books Limited 1988
A member of the Namara Group
27/29 Goodge Street
London W1P 1FD

Copyright © by Jose Villiers 1988

British Library Cataloguing in Publication Data

Villiers, Lady Jose
    Granny was a spy.
    1. Belgium. Social life, 1939-1945.
    Personal observations
    I. Title
    949.3'042'0924

ISBN 0 7043 2683 3

Typeset by Reprotype Limited, Peterborough, Cambs
Printed and bound in Great Britain by
The Camelot Press Plc, Southampton

'Hurum Gallorum fortissimae sunt Belgae'
(Of all the Gauls, the Belgae were the bravest)

Julius Caesar, De Bello Gallico

Acknowledgements

This book would not have been possible without the help of Richard Passmore, who has devoted so much time to doing research and helping me to write. My thanks are also due to Mrs Ann Mills for typing out the manuscript while having to decipher my handwriting, and to the Imperial War Museum for supplying much background material.

Contents

Preface

My nine-year-old grandson, Toby, went out jogging with some American friends. On their return one of them told me, 'Toby said, did you know my Granny was a spy?' They started to ask questions and I realized that, apart from passing references, I had not talked to my grandchildren, nor even to my children, about my experiences during the war years. Even when prodded I hesitated about those years, so much time had elapsed. However, I remembered a box in the attic where I had left the notes I made when I arrived in London in March 1943, and the photographs which I had kept for their significance.

With these papers to jog my memory I started to write this short account of my life between 1938 and 1947. To complete the tale I went to Belgium to see old friends with whom I had worked, and the Belgian Centre for Research and Historical Study on the Second World War was most helpful. I feel that this is the time to put a few stories on record before fading memory makes it all too difficult. That is the reason why I have written these pages. Also, it has occurred to me that most young people know very little about the war and do not understand the suffering and hardship their forebears had to undergo. Even the name 'Hitler' is not always familiar to them.

I dedicate this book to my friends and companions who died in concentration camps, and to those who suffered great hardships.

I write this also for my grandchildren, Toby, Lara, Marina and Alexandra, in the hope that they will have a peaceful life, but to urge them always to fight aggression and dictatorship if need be. These stories will, of course, seem unsophisticated to children brought up in an electronic age, but we were trying to do our best with what we knew at the time. I hope they would do the same.

M.J.V.

NORTH SEA
OOSTENDE
DUNKERQUE
LE ZOUTE
DE PANNE
NIEUWPOORT
WESTENDE
BRUGES
HOLLAND
BREDA
YPRES
GHENT
MELLE
schelde
Deurne
ANTWERP
COURTRAI
Berchem
EINDHOVEN
LILLE
MECHELEN
Albert Canal
Laeken
CHIÈVRES
BRUSSELS
WAVRE
HASSELT
maas
MONS
BOUSSU
CAMBRAI
GEMBLOUX
MAASTRICHT
meuse
NAMUR
LIEGE
AACHEN
NORTH
Philippeville
DINANT
BELGIUM
FRANCE
SEDAN
ARDENNES
GERMANY
LUXEMBOURG
meuse
VERDUN

1

The Calm and the Storm

'NEVER forget,' my father sometimes warned us children, 'that the Boche invaded Belgium once, and if it ever suits their purpose, they will come here again.' The Boche were, of course, the Germans, and we would press my father for details of the occupation years of World War One. In those days, of course, we called it 'La Grande Guerre'. Like all children, we derived an unholy satisfaction from the grim details of the hardships, the destruction and the atrocities – and seconds later would be dashing madly around the grounds of the château, war totally forgotten, wholly immersed in some childish diversion. Yet before I was far into my teens I had a fair understanding of what had happened to our people in the years 1914 to 1918.

Then, it will be recalled, Germany issued an ultimatum to Belgium in contravention of its pledge to respect, and even defend, her neutrality. When that ultimatum was refused, Germany invaded, *en route* for northern France. We children knew only too well of the six hundred citizens shot in the market square at Dinant – presumably by way of revenge for the fierce defence of the town put up by the retreating Belgian forces – after which Dinant was sacked. We knew of the floods of refugees who fled to England, largely colonizing such places as Richmond-on-Thames with such success that some worthy Belgian citizens elected to stay in England after the war had ended. We knew by heart, from frequent repetition, the words of King Albert in 1914: 'A country which defends itself commands the respect of all; that country does not perish.' So we were in no doubt what war had meant; as we grew older, therefore, we lived under the shadow of what a new war would bring – yet life went on.

We lived at Jurbise, near Mons, in a château: it was a large, grey,

1

stone-built place, its harsh outline softened by the wistaria and the other colourful creepers which covered it for most of the year. There were two terraces of climbing roses, a wealth of rich colour during the summer months and well into the autumn; there were also well-tended beds of flowers all around and the grounds were a joy to the eye. Not far away was the little village of Jurbise itself, and we children knew well every stone of it and were friendly with many of the inhabitants. Compared with the other châteaux in the area ours was not, in fact, very large; but with its many bedrooms and fine reception rooms, it was a much-loved family home.

My parents, the Comte and Comtesse de la Barre, went to live there after the death of my paternal grandparents: for this purpose they left Calehill Park, in Kent, the English home of my mother's family. Here the family had settled in 1914 to escape the German occupation of our country, while my father served with the British Army in Flanders, and here they lived happily until their return to Belgium after the end of the war.

My elder sister, Béatrice, had been born in Belgium before the family left; my brother John and I were born in England during the war years. My other brothers were born in Belgium, after 1919. We were a large, affectionate and closely-knit family; at home we were completely bilingual, speaking English often with my mother and French with my father. At table, or whenever else the family was together, conversation took the form of an amusing Franglais – a word not then invented; we delighted in incongruities, and sentences composed at random of English and French words caused much laughter. Life was indeed happy then.

Jurbise was very much my home; I thought only rarely and fleetingly of Kent – after all, I was barely three when we returned to Belgium. The village was a bucolic place, full of rural noises and smells, in the Walloon area of Belgium. The park surrounding the château was well stocked with trees and lakes and favourite walks, a blissful place for growing children. In the summer we swam a great deal and in the winter we skated. We were looked after by a governess (for the older children) and a nanny (for the younger children), together with several *domestiques*, who were, we felt, very much part of the family.

Our happy childhood was sometimes clouded by unhappy episodes with the current nanny or 'keeper'. One, who will remain nameless, was a particular bane to us. Her discipline was harsh and enforced, when she considered it necessary, by a stick. Once, I remember, John offended

2

her in some way and she put him inside a linen basket and secured the lid. His cries were disturbing in the extreme – to us. Towards myself she was more guarded: on one early occasion I had picked up a steel bar and threatened her with immediate retaliation; from that time on she was clearly wary of my possible reaction to any punishment she might wish to inflict. Eventually, inevitably, we had to tell our parents, and she had to go. Her successor was an Irish girl called Eileen; we were quite fond of her, but as the months went by she began to show signs of some emotional disorder. She would walk the corridors at night, weeping and crying that the Black and Tans were coming for her. Eventually she had to be returned to her family. We missed her very much, especially her stories of leprechauns and fairies.

Another nanny, who was engaged to look after my younger brother Philippe and was large, comfortable, placid and middle-aged, took to the bottle and would occasionally tether Philippe to a seat in the garden by means of a long cord, so that she could indulge in a drinking-bout. For a time nobody – no adult, that is – seemed to notice this, but one day she was found to be dead-drunk in her room; a large cache of empty gin bottles was found under her bed. So she too had to go.

Father, although dearly loved, was a distant figure; his work as a senator took him to Brussels during the week and many of his evenings were spent in looking after his constituency – when he was not busily involved in his other function as Burgomeister of Jurbise. Mother we did at least see every evening, but our days were spent under the direct control of the current governess and the nursemaids, and so to us they were more immediately important figures. Until I reached the age of eleven I was taught at home by teachers from the local school (which had been founded many years before by my grandfather). Like my brothers and sister, I was taught enough literature, history, geography and mathematics to get by – though in the case of the last subject, only just enough. We had many friends and neighbours with whom we played tennis and had fun at weekends, staying in each other's houses. Despite this carefree life-style, however, we were not really wealthy; home comforts had priority on the family purse and we children were not given much pocket money or many nice clothes. Often I would borrow from a friend some lovely dress, so that I might look my best at a party.

One of my happiest memories of those days at Jurbise is of the dogs we owned. The first was an Alsatian; he and I were quite inseparable. Then there was a cross-breed of some kind, large but beautiful; I called him McNab. These dogs were supposed, by a stern edict, not to be

3

allowed up to my bedroom, but when the house was quiet at night I would give a low whistle and McNab would rush very quietly up two floors to join me. He knew well enough that this was not allowed and that he must not be seen on his way up, but the rug at the foot of my bed was his favourite sleeping-place. One day, unfortunately, my regular maid (who knew of our reprehensible conduct, and connived at it by smuggling McNab downstairs in the morning) was ill and her temporary replacement came in at the usual time of 7.30 a.m. to draw back the curtains and make sure that I was awake. McNab knew her not: with a threatening growl he leapt at her and she retreated hastily with fearful shrieks which awoke everyone – including my parents. After this episode McNab was officially escorted to the cloakroom each night, to our mutual disappointment.

We owned two cars. The first was a large Minerva; it wore with conscious pride a pair of parliamentary number-plates, P11, which constituted a great distinction, setting it apart from most other road-users. The Minerva would be driven only by my father or a chauffeur; when we children were permitted to join Father on occasional journeys, we were very conscious of the glances, curious or respectful, evoked by the magnificent car, its chauffeur and, especially, its number-plates. The second car was a two-seater Citroën with a dicky-seat at the rear; this car was a source of infinite, if illicit, joy to my brother Alain and myself. We used to drive it around the park and even, quite illegally, out into the main road. We were both, of course, considerably below the age at which the law permitted us to drive on the public highway, and when my father heard that we had been driving outside the park (and in some mysterious way he often *did* hear), we had to endure a tremendous dressing-down. Alain and I, nevertheless, both considered ourselves capable drivers, though when (as often happened) I stalled the engine, only Alain was strong enough to crank it into action again.

Wisely, my father wanted us to realize early in our lives that ours was a privileged pattern of existence. On several occasions he arranged for us to go down one or other of the coal-mines in the Borinage, part of his constituency, to see the conditions under which the miners had to work. I was very impressed and mildly intimidated by the scenes underground: the long galleries, feebly illuminated by occasional lamps, and the pit ponies pulling laden trucks. I did not like crawling along the low and narrow seams: some latent claustrophobia would stir. Often there would be an ominous crack as one of the timber pit-props warned us that one day ... I was really frightened, but the miners merely laughed. I was

4

perpetually surprised at their confidence. When at last we emerged into the daylight again, with blackened faces and red eyes, I always felt a great sense of relief, together with mingled sympathy and admiration for the men who descended several hundred feet daily to their dangerous work. We often visited their families and were always made very welcome; sometimes it was our sad duty to offer our sympathy after a pit accident, and such accidents were much more frequent in those days than they are now.

Eventually, of course, the halcyon days had to end: it was decided that I was old enough to go off to a boarding school. So I was sent to the Convent of the Assumption in Mons. Here I was an unsatisfactory pupil. At the subjects I enjoyed I worked well enough; but other subjects I neglected shamelessly. And always I was up to some kind of mischief: picnics after lights-out, which usually betrayed themselves by uncontrollable hilarity; or sorties to the roof, by means of a skylight in the attic (itself forbidden territory), in order to have races up there under the night sky. At times I would put a frog into a lavatory bowl, much to the distress of the good nuns who did not receive my happy nonsense well. My older sister, Béatrice, was awarded the good conduct ribbon – a much-coveted distinction in that hothouse atmosphere. I never came anywhere near being even considered for that decoration. But I had many friends among the other girls and enjoyed playing games, *official* games: tennis and netball. So those few years were not, on balance, unhappy. Later I spent a year studying art, after which I was sent to England, the country of my birth, to be 'finished' at a school in Haywards Heath.

After this my education was considered to be complete and I returned to Belgium. There followed the years of 'coming out': dancing through the night – perhaps thirty such nights in succession. We were all happily caught up in the glamorous social whirl; hostesses would rival each other to see who could put on the most splendid dance and those of us who were lucky enough, or pretty enough, would stagger sleepily home at dawn, clutching an armful of flowers. At that time it was the custom for young men to present bouquets to the girls who took their fancy. I enjoyed many innocent flirtations but was wholly determined that they would be transient: it was far too early, I considered, for anything more serious and lasting.

Life was so full and so happy that I almost forgot my father's earlier warnings: yet to the south of our glamorous world (and not so very far south, either) a resurgent nation was rediscovering its pride, its strength and its age-old conviction of its historical role on the world stage. My sister and I were now living partly in Jurbise and partly in Brussels, at the magnificent townhouse of our grandparents, the Marquis and Marquise du Parc, on the Avenue Louise. Their many servants looked after us devotedly and it took an enormous mental effort to remind ourselves that as a way of life ours was wholly unrealistic. It was certainly no kind of preparation for the hard times which were even then ahead of us all. Yet reality did break through: the occasional newspaper or radio bulletin pierced our beautiful illusion and we knew that Belgium might well once again find herself involved in a war not of her making.

My sister Béatrice and I agreed that we ought to make ourselves ready to play a useful part should trouble once again come to our country. After some discussion we reached a decision and one day in late 1938 we applied to join the Motor Corps, an ambulance unit even then being formed by the Red Cross. In the event of an invasion, the young women of the Corps would drive cars and ambulances; to fit them for this, they would be trained in vehicle maintenance, map-reading and first-aid. As part of that training, the two of us were attached to the Brussels Ambulance Service; even now, so many years after, I remember vividly my first day with them.

As might be imagined, I was very nervous at the prospect of, say, having to retrieve the remains of someone who had been run over by one of the trams which criss-crossed Brussels in those years and which were frequently involved in accidents – more or less messy. So I sat in the ready-room, my heart pounding and my mouth dry, despite frequent cups of coffee. I fidgeted nervously and jumped involuntarily every time the telephone rang. Then our call came. It was not a street accident (no blood, mercifully) but an elderly man who had suffered a heart attack. We set off, bells ringing, and carved our way through the traffic (this was really quite exciting, after all). We found our patient, laid him on a stretcher and loaded him carefully into the ambulance, watched by a curious crowd; then we set off again dramatically for the hospital. At a crossroads, wham! a car crashed into our ambulance and we toppled over on to one side; our unfortunate patient was hurled to the floor. He was barely conscious but once I had untangled myself from him – both of us lying in the side of our ill-fated vehicle – I was able to help get him out and back on to his stretcher. I was no longer pleasurably excited: I was badly shaken. Another ambulance was called and eventually got our patient to the peace of a hospital. By then I was beginning to feel that I needed a spell in the next bed myself but was given to understand that such happenings were all in a day's work; in fact, there might be worse, and even much worse, ahead. So ended my first day's training. Succeeding days were mercifully less demanding – at least, for another eighteen months or so.

By now I was twenty-two and with each day that passed I became increasingly conscious of the unease which loomed over Europe, like a menacing cloud. In September 1938 came the Munich Agreement between Hitler, Mussolini, Daladier and Chamberlain; in some quarters this was hailed as 'peace in our time' (a phrase from the Anglican *Book of Common Prayer*); in Belgium, however, we looked cynically upon the Agreement, regarding it – as indeed it turned out to be – as merely a stay of execution. The clouds of war, we believed, could only get darker until the inevitable outbreak. Following the occupation of the Sudetenland, inhabited largely by ethnic Germans, terrible stories began to filter out: of Jewish houses, shops and synagogues being burned, of many Jews either being killed or disappearing. When, six months later, Germany invaded and dismembered the rump state of Czechoslovakia, none of us was the least surprised: Hitler's 'last territorial claim' had been anything but his last. In which direction, we wondered, would he reach out next?

Britain and France, on whom Belgium looked as elder sisters as it were, reacted to the rape of Czechoslovakia with comparatively feeble verbal objections. Then they took an exasperated and fateful step. On 31 March 1939 the Allies formally guaranteed that they would defend the frontiers of Poland, the next potential victim of Nazi aggression. This step might well have halted the slide to war: even Hitler could not have accepted the risk of a war on two fronts – for the Soviet Union could not be indifferent to a German conquest of Poland. But then came the bombshell: the Nazi–Soviet Pact (not mentioned in Soviet 'histories' of today). War was now inevitable. The Allies, in desperation, repeated their pledge to Poland, but the writing was clearly on the wall, and we were all conscious of it. How could the Allies fulfil their pledge without involving all Europe, and perhaps most of the world, in a war?

A few days after the signing of the Pact, German troops invaded Poland and once again Europe was, or soon would be, at war.

That winter of 1939–40 was an especially anxious time for us. Britain and France were at war with Germany and, further east, Poland had been coldbloodedly divided between Germany and the Soviet Union.

True, the war on land was quiescent, but it could break out in all its force at any moment; France had its – supposedly impregnable – Maginot Line, which it was now feverishly extending along the Franco-Belgian frontier to the sea – but, as events soon proved, too late. It was obvious that once more, as in a previous war, Germany's way into France would be via Belgium; the only question was, when? Our government still tried to convince us and itself that Belgium could remain neutral, but few people were convinced. Some 500,000 men were called up and most of them were sent to guard the frontier – one could not speak of fortifications – facing Germany. Overnight, many of our friends vanished from the scene and my brother John was a lieutenant in the 1st Regiment of Guides. The Guides had been a cavalry unit but were not equipped with armoured cars; John's unit was stationed somewhere on the frontier, where they exercised and prepared for the inevitable day. Occasionally, John would manage to get home for a few days' leave, and it was good to see the whole family together again – I often managed to get to Jurbise myself when he was at home. Yet we were all conscious of the underlying menace and my parents were always clearly sad when once again we had to see John off on his return to his unit.

In public John always assumed a quiet confidence – mainly, I think, to spare my mother and sister anxiety. What he said to my father in private I have, of course, no idea. But one day, I remember, when he and I were alone, I asked, 'If they do attack us, can we really stop them?' He looked serious. 'Hardly,' he answered. 'At best we can delay them until the Allies arrive. But part of Belgium will inevitably be occupied again. There are too many of them. They are too well equipped. They have had a lot of practice and they believe they are invincible. And perhaps they really are. But don't worry: we'll try to solve our problems as they happen.'

So I tried not to worry but I put increased conviction into every aspect of my training with the Ambulance Corps. Perhaps the family would retreat to England again until the war was over and Germany was defeated? (There was no question whatever of what the outcome of the war had to be – somehow.) But Father was a senator and would never consider leaving the country, whatever happened; John was already in the army; Alain had not yet been called up but he was of an age and would certainly be conscripted once the war came to Belgium; even Xavier was not so far below military age. All in all, it was a time when each of us had cause to worry, yet each of us kept those worries private: in public we always spoke of other, happier, things.

8

The months crawled by. The Germans used the interval to wage a massive propaganda war, to undermine the will to resist – not only of its official enemies, Britain and France, but of the neutrals too. Dr Goebbels, a master of deception by plausible lies and half-truths, constantly proclaimed Germany's beneficent intentions. On many evenings, at Jurbise or back with the Ambulance Unit, or wherever I happened to be, I listened to the radio and thought of our many friends in the army; we all listened daily to the BBC – and waited. My father's earlier warnings were acquiring day by day a new significance. In response to the deluge of enemy propaganda, the French reacted bravely enough: their press and radio were full of assurances that they could and would deal with the German aggressor. But France, as all too soon became obvious, was a divided nation. Many walls in Paris carried the graffito, 'Pour qui et pourquoi?' Marxist propaganda among working people had had its effect. The French Confédération Général du Travail – the equivalent of the British TUC – was Communist-dominated, and the world-wide Communist line, following the signing of the Russo-German pact, was to urge the workers not to support the war. In this way, Russia's ally, Nazi Germany, would be helped to victory. Inevitably, such sentiments infected some units of the French armed forces. When, later, the Wehrmacht approached Paris, the French army fought bitterly, but the awakening came too late.

The French and Belgian secret services had long been aware that the Germans intended to attack the Allies through Holland and Belgium, and this was confirmed when a German courier plane, an Me 108, made a forced landing in Belgium on 10 January 1940. On board were two senior officers: the pilot, Major Hoenmans, who had served in the First World War, and his passenger, Major Helmuth Reinberger of the Fallschirmjäger, German paratroops, who was carrying highly secret documents. One of the two had wanted to wangle a night to visit his mistress and in order to make up the time they had decided to come from Münster to Cologne by air instead of by train. The weather forecast was good.

At first all went well but later, as often happens in the Ruhr Valley, a thick fog came down on the countryside and the pilot, lacking experience of the area and realizing that the aircraft was running low on fuel, decided to put down somewhere and wait for the fog to clear. Unfortunately for him, he had mistaken the Meuse for the Rhine, and they landed in a field at Mechelen, in Belgium. Some soldiers who were stationed nearby rushed over; at first they found only one man, in a German uniform; but then they were alerted by smoke rising behind a hedge. There

9

they found a second German, trying desperately to destroy some papers. The soldiers stamped out the fire, arrested both Germans and seized the papers. The party then went to a nearby farmhouse where they phoned for transport. The two German officers then requested that they might ring their families to assure them of their safety, but they were told that the Belgian authorities would see to that. A Belgian security officer, who arrived before very long realized the importance of the papers: they contained detailed orders for an attack on Holland, Belgium and Luxembourg. Belgian army headquarters were informed immediately.

While they waited, Major Hoenmans asked to be allowed to use the lavatory; under cover of the general movement and distraction, Major Reinberger grabbed the papers, dashed to the stove and thrust them in. Immediately, the Belgian officer retrieved them, burning his hand as he did so; the papers, although singed, were perfectly legible. Reinberger now broke down. He grabbed the pistol of the Belgian officer from its holster and raised it to his own head, intending to commit suicide. There was a brief and violent struggle and the gun was wrested from him. The German then struck his head violently and repeatedly against the wall of the room, moaning in total despair, 'I have lost my honour.'

The Belgian newspapers all carried news of the forced landing but were not told the contents of the papers and so they attached little importance to the incident; certainly, when we read the account at the time we could not guess the significance of the episode. Now we know that Berlin, alarmed by the newspaper reports, ordered Oberst Von Pappenheim, the military attaché in Brussels, to seek an interview with the two interned officers. When the attaché met his compatriots he did so in a room which, in the jargon of a later age, had been bugged. The attaché asked the Belgian officer present to supply him with writing materials, and when this man left the room to fetch them, the internees were asked whether the papers had been destroyed.

'Yes,' was the answer from both officers.

The importance of this affair was underlined in two other ways. The papal nuncio, Monsignor Micara,* let it be known that there were strong indications, presumably via Italian military circles, of German intentions. Then a high official of the Italian Foreign Office warned Princess Marie José, a sister of King Leopold and the wife of Crown Prince Umberto, that the war was coming to Belgium in the near future. She managed to communicate this to King Leopold. The British and French

*Later Cardinal Micara.

military attachés were kept informed of all these events, and King Leopold asked for an interview with Admiral Keyes, so that he, too, might be briefed.

Although, according to the Hague Convention, Belgium was entitled to intern the two German officers, they were quickly sent home to Germany. Clearly the Belgian government wanted to do nothing that would cause any friction, however minor, with the Germans. On their return the two officers swore that the documents had been destroyed but Hitler, perhaps detecting contradictions in their separate accounts, did not believe them. Both men were later shot.

The German plan of attack was therefore switched: the main thrust would now be against the French positions at Sedan. This, of course, we found out only much later; the French, however, were convinced that the Germans would hold to their original plans, revealed by the captured documents: they placed the main part of their army on the Belgian frontier, thus fatally weakening their defensive capability at Sedan. When, in May 1940, the Germans broke through in that sector, the fate of the Western Allies was decided.

Large parts of this story came into the possession of my father and so the atmosphere of anticipation at home intensified as the weeks went by. If – when – the Germans invaded, my brother John would be in the thick of the fighting; knowing of German methods at Warsaw, we could only fear greatly for our own cities and dread that a similar destruction could come to us, too.

There were of course those among us who felt and professed sympathy for the German cause. Leon Degrelle and his followers, the Rexistes, were open followers of the Nazi line and were vociferous in their advocacy of the New Order. (Here it might be timely to look ahead. By 1945 the Rexistes realized that their cause was lost. In revenge they tried to assassinate several well-known people, including my father, who had to go into hiding until the arrival of Allied forces. Degrelle is at the time of writing [1987] in Spain, having taken Spanish nationality. Recently he broadcast a flat denial that the Nazis had been guilty either of war crimes or of the atrocities in the concentration camps.) I must confess that I was mildly attracted to the Nuremberg-type rallies of the Rexistes and was half convinced by their eloquence, but my father warned me repeatedly against the fine words which masked reality. 'What a politician says and what he means are often two different things,' my father said. 'That is especially true of the fanatics on both wings of the political spectrum.' I had enormous respect for my father's political

11

wisdom and thereafter viewed the Rexistes much more critically.

After so many months of fearful anticipation, the reality came on 10 May 1940, a date which will live long in many memories – as significant a date as 4 August 1914. We were awoken, that lovely, sunny morning, by the sound of bombs dropping on the outskirts of Brussels; very soon, our anti-aircraft guns joined in. With a complex shiver – excitement, fear, disbelief – we realized that this finally was war: the great reality had arrived. Thinking back to that fine spring morning, I doubt that many people foresaw that we would hear those same noises for many more days and, especially, nights to come. Dressing hurriedly, we made what preparations we could. The windows we criss-crossed with sticky tape to avoid glass splinters should they shatter from a near miss (if it was worse than a near miss, of course, a few glass splinters wouldn't matter much in the general destruction). A blackout was improvised. We filled the bath with water, in case of fire.

The radio, which we now kept permanently turned on, was giving out continuous reports of the unprovoked and unannounced attack on our country; we were heartened to hear that, at the request of our government, British and French forces were pouring across the frontier, on the way to meet the invading German army. Our own army, we were realistic enough to know, would be heavily outnumbered and unable to hold quite inadequate defensive positions – the result of Belgium's declared policy of total neutrality in the past years.

When we had done what we could, we donned our uniforms, Béatrice and I; she must have felt, as I did, that this time and at last it was for real. Then we went off to report for duty with the Motor Corps. We agreed that we felt we were only playing at soldiers, even now: the war was still 'la guerre fraîche et joyeuse', but this enthusiasm and inordinate optimism were soon to fade in the face of grim reality and the need for tenacity.

As I entered the ambulance station, my friend Régine said, 'Well, this is it. Do you think it will be like 1914 all over again?'

I must admit that I half feared that it would but it would have been defeatist to have said so there and then. With more confidence than I really felt, I replied, 'The British and the French are on the way by now. We're all in it together.' It wasn't really an answer but there was, fortunately, no time to go into supplementary detail; no sooner had we reported in than we were ordered to go at once to Antwerp to collect new ambulances which had just been handed over there. So we set off, dividing our attention between the road in front and the sky above. As we neared Berchem we saw several houses burning: the German bombers had already left their calling cards. People were running this way and that in a confused manner; as we slowed to negotiate the cluttered streets we could see that many of the civilians – mostly women and older men – looked dazed. Ambulances and fire-engines were dashing about, their bells adding dramatically to the high level of noise and confusion. The sky was now full of aircraft; we hoped that these were Allied aircraft, come to help us, but alas, they were all German: troop-carrying Ju 52s, and Ju 87s – the dreaded Stukas. These latter, we found, had the job of attacking key road junctions, rail targets and all kinds of bridges. At such tasks they were terribly efficient. Their dive-bombing technique guaranteed a high degree of accuracy and the sirens attached to their fixed undercarriages instilled the maximum of fear in the areas around their targets. Anyone who heard that banshee-wail, rising in pitch and volume as the aircraft dropped like a stone, almost vertically, will never forget it. We cowered but overcame our fear and threaded a path carefully through and around the numerous obstacles. Smaller aircraft, which we later learned to recognize as Me 110s, roamed the countryside at will, diving here and there to use their cannons and machine-guns on selected targets – and not always military ones. Their intention was to cause panic and to block roads so that they were impassable to our military convoys; soon we were having to pick our way past the dreadful results of their work.

It was a dramatic introduction to the reality of total war and, as might be expected, we were all frightened and excited at the same time. This was precisely what all our training had been about; despite our cold shivers, we felt that we were being useful at last, and the others must have been as determined as I was – no matter what came, I would somehow carry on.

Eventually we reached Antwerp and collected our ambulances; we checked them for fuel, oil and water then drove them away. By now it was late afternoon and we were ordered to go back to Brussels and to wait there at the Gare du Nord for an expected trainload of refugees from the areas further north-east. Luckily, the return journey was less eventful: we seemed to have found a lull in the bombing and we could see that the various rescue services were gradually sorting out the chaos. With two of my friends, Régine le Boeuf and Princesse Antoinette de Ligne, I parked outside the station and waited. Nobody seemed to know when 'our' train would arrive: railway services that day were largely subject to improvisation rather than time-tables. The forecourt of the

13

station was densely packed with people – once again mainly women, the very young and the very old. Then we heard the first ominous noises and, looking up, we saw the first of a formation of Stukas already commencing his dive; his followers were about to peel off one by one and follow him.

Immediately there was panic. Many people rushed towards a narrow, underground tunnel; it was plain that we had the makings of a very unpleasant accident when that fear-crazed crowd tried to press its way into that narrow entrance. Régine, however, saw clearly what had to be done. She shouted to me but in the confusion and the din I could not make out what it was she was saying; then by yelling and waving her arms vigorously she managed to turn the crowd into the hall of a nearby hotel. The doorway was very wide, and as the people crowded inside, the staff directed them down into the cellars. Safely – we hoped – tucked away underground we waited anxiously; the crump of the bombs was enough to inspire fear, even in the cellar: some women wept and small children screamed. However, the raid was soon over and we emerged into daylight to find some damage nearby but not as much as we had feared. The station, at least, seemed to be still in working order and our ambulances were undamaged.

The bombing had further delayed our train, however, and it was late evening before our casualties arrived. First came the badly wounded, followed by those less seriously injured and then the women and children. Finally came the old people, who had been evacuated from their homes as the tide of battle flooded in their direction. All of them seemed totally bewildered by the march of events.

I was given charge of a little girl, perhaps five years old, who was bleeding quite badly from injuries to an arm and both legs. She had had emergency dressings which now needed changing. With her were her mother and a very old man, who might even have been the mother's grandfather. I took them to another Brussels station and their journey continued, to hoped-for safety – perhaps in France. It was my first close contact with refugees and as I carried the little girl, as gently as I could, I was filled with compassion for her and a total hatred against the country which had, twice in a lifetime, deliberately and without provocation, created such misery for the innocent and helpless.

The blackout that evening, our first, was a new experience and one which caused us drivers great difficulty. The once-familiar streets were now dark canyons and the buildings on either side, unlighted cliffs. We went backwards and forwards, meeting trainload after trainload of refugees; they were all feverishly agitated and terribly frightened; they found comfort in moving in masses, impelled by some primal herd instinct and not knowing where they were going to or why. They were resigned to constant journeying, hoping in a dull way that at the end of the last journey there would be stability after chaos. Their plight was made more difficult by constantly changing orders, which stopped or started trains quite unpredictably, or which switched scheduled trains from one destination to another at the shortest notice.

Military reservists, called up and now trying to reach their units, were often at a loss; the station staff were usually in no position to help. Altogether, it was a picture of complete chaos which those who experienced that day will never be able to forget.

In all the bustle at the station I suddenly realized that standing near me was a man whom I recognized as the German Ambassador, von Bülow-Schwante, now returning to his own country by way of neutral Switzerland. I had a strong impulse to go up to him and tell him my opinion of the *Herrenvolk* of whom he was so proud; but the presence of my uncle, the Vicomte de Ghellink, who was the chief of protocol, kept me back. He would be held responsible for any unpleasantness of which the outgoing ambassador might have cause to complain. So I waved and smiled at my uncle and ignored his protégé of the moment.

Our Motor Corps, so painstakingly built up and trained over the past two years, was now proving its worth. The days following that fateful 10 May were very busy for us; so busy in fact, that there was very little chance for me to worry about my family – let alone try to get in touch. Life was simply work and sleep: overmuch of the one and not enough of the other. We learned to cat-nap at any available moment and under whatever circumstances. We travelled all over the country to bring blood supplies to hospitals and to ferry wounded people and refugees. We were quietly glad to be so busy and so useful, even though at the end of each day we collapsed on to the nearest bed, wherever we happened to be, and fell into an exhausted sleep.

All sorts of rumours were circulating. The Albert Canal was holding; the Germans had crossed it; such and such a regiment had suffered severe casualties; the Germans had penetrated the French front at Sedan and would soon overrun us all. We just did not know what to believe so we disbelieved every rumour and got on with our work. The radio was not much help: reports tended to contradict each other and were, in any case, guarded. One of the most disturbing rumours was of German paratroops being dropped all over the country in disguise –

15

even, it was said, descending on central Brussels in the guise of nuns. Of course, nobody had actually *seen* them, but everyone had a cousin or a friend who was supposed to have done so.

Such rumours gave rise to considerable confusion on the roads as regular police, or auxiliaries equipped only with armbands, stopped cars to check on the identity of the drivers. At night one often encountered agitated men brandishing revolvers and shouting at us to stop – or else! It was obviously wise to do nothing which might trigger off hysteria: fortunately, an ambulance driven by a young woman was the least suspicious of vehicles.

One day, I remember, I helped to evacuate the sanatorium at Tombeek, near Wavre, which was thought to be too near the Allied line – if indeed there was such a line. Françoise May, Loulou de Wouters and I were sent with the only three vehicles then available. To make as much progress as possible before dark we cracked on at speed, often meeting British columns moving this way or that. The Belgian people always welcomed the British with joy and exuberant enthusiasm, to which the Tommies returned a thumbs-up sign. That day there were pockets of sporadic fighting here and there, people were still being killed and wounded, but we soon reached Tombeek and sat beside our ambulances, waiting for the patients to be brought out and loaded. Suddenly the air-raid siren started up. We all froze. The sanatorium was a conspicuous building on top of a hill and completely exposed.

'Are you frightened?' asked one of my friends in a low voice (in case the crews of the bombers heard!).

'I'm scared to death,' I replied honestly. 'Tell you what: let's break out the emergency rations, shall we?'

'Well,' she said, shakily, 'it really *is* an emergency.'

So we took a sip of brandy and waited, both determined not to give way to our fear. Soon the first patients were ready and, assisted by several other ambulances and cars which had now joined us, we made frequent trips to Brussels. By one o'clock the following morning I was taking my last load from Tombeek when somewhere along the road I realized that I was caught up in an unlit British military column. This was difficult, to put it mildly. Although my headlights were so masked as to be very nearly useless, every time I braked the braking lights would shine brightly. Despite the shouts of obvious outrage, I dared not stop: the road would have been completely blocked. So I tried to drive very slowly and carefully, paying regard to minimum visibility and using the foot-brake as little as possible. Suddenly a motorcycle appeared along-

16

side my cab; the MP riding it swore bitterly at me (my finishing school at Haywards Heath had enlarged my education in more ways than the staff there had realized) about the braking lights. At that moment there was the noise of aircraft engines and an unmistakable tic-tac on the surface of the road: we were being machine-gunned. There was an extra-loud bang as a bullet pierced the bodywork of the car I was driving. The MP flashed his torch briefly in my face and saw that I was a girl. At once he changed his tone and said, 'Don't worry, miss: just follow me! I could have hugged him. Eventually we were clear of the column and away but, as we found later, two of my patients had died. At dawn I returned to base, to find that Béatrice had had an equally fraught time. She had spent much of the previous day at railway stations, waiting for and subsequently transporting the endless numbers of wounded. The sirens howled almost continuously as one air-raid succeeded another, and stations were not safe places to be at such times: Stukas and Me 110s roamed at will and a crowd of refugees or wounded and ambulances (marked clearly as such) constituted a tempting target. The Red Cross, apparently, meant nothing to German airmen.

For several more days and nights the Motor Corps was sent to destinations all over our shrinking country, often strafed by passing German aircraft which sought to block the roads to all military traffic. After a column of refugees had been thus attacked the road would be littered with the dead and wounded and with dead and dying horses, overturned vehicles of all kinds and every variety of household goods. On one occasion I found myself near Philippeville, in the province of Namur, and here I met French troops for the first time. They were smartly turned out and seemed very optimistic about the immediate future; indeed, at that time the French army enjoyed a tremendously high reputation. Few could have foreseen its imminent disarray; certainly I did not.

Chasing this way and that across the countryside, we knew little of events outside our own small and mobile world. By 17 May the government had left Brussels, delegating to various territorial *départements* powers for the continuance of essential administration. Some *secrétaires-général*, whose portfolios included domestic affairs, were asked to remain at their posts in Brussels, to avoid a complete dislocation of central government – but some of these people disobeyed orders and left. The ensuing confusion nationwide bordered on anarchy. The Burgomeister of Brussels, F.J. van de Meulebroeck, stayed at his post; he issued a proclamation to the citizens urging calm and dignity, and asking them to stay indoors when the Germans arrived and to abstain from all provocation, injury or threats to enemy troops. He asked for the confidence of the people and said, 'Whatever the duration of the test may be, all Belgians should have as their watchwords: "Fors le Roi, nul ne sert!"* This was on 16 May, less than a week after the Wehrmacht had attacked us, so the speed of the German advance was obvious. We were unaware of these developments, however, as only scattered fragments of hard news came our way and, in truth, were of secondary importance to our more immediate duties.

From its temporary headquarters the Belgian government now issued an order that all men between the ages of eighteen and thirty-five, who had not yet been called up, should go to Ypres; if this was not possible, they should make for the coast. These men would be collected and assigned to a Belgian unit now forming in France. They would then be trained for service in the Belgian army. This proclamation caused numbers of men to home-in on Ypres from every direction; the congestion thus caused on roads and railways was made worse by large numbers of civilians trying to reach safe areas in north and north-west Belgium. In the Great War, the territory here had never been occupied by the Germans; King Albert and Queen Elizabeth had lived at La Panne until the end of that war, and now people believed that history would repeat itself. Alas for our illusions! Panic is not easily stilled and it is infectious; in many cases families who had reached a reasoned decision to stay in their homes and await events would suddenly pack a few bags with objects incongruously chosen and flee. Our ambulances would not have been able to function on the congested roads were it not for the fact that the British army had designated some main routes as being for military traffic only and our ambulances and cars were given permission to use these roads.

One day I was driving through Melle when I saw, for the first time, a Belgian AA battery open fire and score a direct hit. The German aircraft – I did not have time to recognize its type – belched black smoke, then nose-dived into the ground not very far away. I could almost feel the vibration as it fell. I could not help thinking of the young men, some mothers' sons, who had just died: my hatred of a few days ago was, for the moment, forgotten. We continued our journey and reached the sea at Westende; there we heard authoritatively that the Germans had broken through the French front at Sedan, which opened dangerous possibilities for the Allied forces still fighting to the north and east who were now in imminent danger of being cut off. Sedan is, of course, just

*Freely translated: 'Do only that which serves the King!'

18

inside the French frontier and a hundred or so miles south of Antwerp. All the Germans had to do now was to press on westwards and then turn north, enclosing what was left of Belgium and all of north-east France in a huge pocket – and that is exactly what they did. Bad news or not, however, we could only dismiss it from our minds and get on with our immediate duties.

We left our wounded in an emergency hospital, a converted hotel at Westende, and I went to find Simone de Biolley, whose husband was serving in the same regiment as my brother John. She had no news of them; all we could do was share our worries – but she did offer me the wonderful comfort of a hot bath after so many hours of arduous driving. Whenever, now, I recall those times, I relive the great solidarity and friendship which existed then; I only wish we had all been able to keep it up. Whenever one of us arrived at the home of a friend, or even a total stranger, we would always be offered hospitality: sometimes a hot meal or the comfort of an armchair in which to rest for a while – or even an improvised mattress on which to snatch an hour or two of desperately needed sleep. One friend of mine sheltered no fewer than eighty-five people in her home, some of them quite unknown to her, within the space of a fortnight, and yet managed to remain wholly unflappable.

On 18 May, a couple of days after van de Meulebroeck's proclamation, we found ourselves on the coast; this time we stayed for two whole days, awaiting orders. When those orders came, we were mildly astonished: we were to cross over into northern France. Perhaps Belgium was to be abandoned to the invader? Certainly, the news being given out by the radio was getting steadily worse. It was a sad convoy of some forty vehicles which eventually drove the few miles along the coastal road and into France; when, I wondered, would we retrace our steps, back into our own country? I think we all felt a pang at leaving Belgium where so many of our relatives and friends now awaited an uncertain, and perhaps dangerous, future. At Bergue, on the frontier, we met a group of Belgian air force pilots; they looked very forlorn and told us that on 10 May, the very first day of hostilities, the German pre-emptive strike had destroyed all their aircraft on the ground; their chances of getting replacements just then were pretty remote.

Eventually the risk of a German encirclement was too obvious to be ignored and we were sent to north-west France. Indeed, by the evening of 20 May and after only ten days' fighting, the German 2nd Panzer Division reached Abbeville, south of Calais, so that all Allied forces to the north were trapped with their backs to the sea. The British escaped the trap by evacuating from Dunkirk and the coast adjacent to it; altogether almost 200,000 British troops, 130,000 French and a few Belgians managed to reach England between 27 May and 4 June. It was an historic and almost a miraculous achievement; even Field Marshal Keitel had grudgingly to admit that Operation Dynamo, as it was called, had been a complete success.

By great good fortune our column managed to escape German encirclement and we made our way steadily south and west. At Gournay-en-Bray, a few miles west of Beauvais, we parked our ambulances: we urgently needed a meal and a rest. People came up to us and told us, 'Radio Stuttgart has already announced the arrival of your ambulance unit and says that the town will be bombed.' They were clearly apprehensive and could not wait for us to continue our journey, so as soon as we could, we left. This sort of thing was cleverly organized by the Germans to unnerve the population in the areas ahead of their advancing spearheads, to increase panic and so lessen the chance of organized resistance. It was a most effective device: wherever we went the local people often begged us to leave their town at once. The fact that the Germans knew so quickly and so accurately of our whereabouts made us wonder about fifth-columnists in our midst; there was no way of knowing who might be serving the enemy in this way and the suspicion served to increase the constant, underlying tension.

As we moved on, we shared the road with a motley collection of vehicles old and new: cars, lorries, horse-drawn farm carts, bicycles, fire-engines, hearses – even desperate women pushing prams, often with a child little older than the baby trudging alongside. In one hearse a baby was born – an odd reversal of the vehicle's role. In their haste to abandon their homes the refugees had taken with them the most extraordinary things: a parrot in its cage, a grandfather clock, a rocking-chair, a dog kennel. Some of the poor souls were dragging themselves along, obviously exhausted, clutching useless objects – perhaps a frying pan. Clearly, they had set out in a blind panic, an emotion strong enough to block off rational thought. It was a heartbreaking procession and more than one of us wept, especially at the sight of unhappy and bewildered children.

We heard about one family, one member of which was a very old aunt. When, once again, the column of refugees was machine-gunned from the air, the aunt was fatally wounded. The family were frantic and undecided: the body could not just be left beside the road: the death had to be registered officially at a *mairie*. Without that there would be legal difficulties in implementing her will, and arrangements must be made for a seemly burial. In desperation, the family rolled the body in two Gobelin tapestries which they had salvaged, secured the bundle to the roof-rack of their car and set off for the nearest town, where they parked the car with its gruesome cargo in a barn overnight. The following day it was indeed still there – but without the tapestries and the dead aunt!

Occasionally the frequent traffic jams and breakdowns had the effect of separating our various vehicles from each other and from our convoy. At one time, I and my co-driver, Antoinette de Ligne, were driving along a minor road in an attempt to by-pass the chaos on the N138. Suddenly a motorcyclist appeared from a side road and shot across our path. There was no way of avoiding him and we hit the motorcycle quite hard, wrecking the bike and hurling the rider in a parabola. When we examined him it was obvious that in addition to shock and minor cuts and bruises he also had a broken leg. We splinted the leg and managed to find a doctor a little further on who took charge of our patient. We resumed our journey but soon realized that in the collision our radiator had been punctured and all our coolant water had leaked away. We were very conscious that the German spearheads were not so far behind and we were desperately anxious not to be overrun. Fortunately, there was a large and imposing house standing a little way back from the road and when we went over to it, we found that the rightful inhabitants had left. So we gained entry, without doing too much damage, and bedded down for the night; our intention was to leave again at first light. We 'borrowed' another car which we found in the garage and which, as fortune would have it, was in full running order, and decided that we would use it to tow our own broken-down car – which was too valuable to abandon. We had, however, no towrope; a detailed search of the house and out-buildings failed to yield any form of rope, so finally we took down the heavy (and expensive) cords of the curtains around windows and used them. They did the job quite adequately and it was, we reassured each other, looting in a good cause. Soon we were able to rejoin our convoy.

All our friends turned out to welcome us back: they had feared the worst. We were especially welcome because Antoinette and I had brought with us a hare which had been caught in our headlights and had failed to take effective evasive action. It was perfectly edible – or would be, when we had time to prepare it. We looked forward to a feast. That night we left the hare casually lying on a desk in the government building which we were occupying. Unfortunately, that particular desk turned out to be one normally used by two particularly sensitive officials who had shown themselves less than brave in the early days of the fighting. On their arrival for work the following morning, they were extremely annoyed to find the hare, which they assumed to be a comment on their behaviour. It took a lot of fervent explanation to make them realize that no criticism had been intended!

By now we were in western France, in an area which, under the terms of the later armistice, was not to be occupied by the Germans and which remained the 'zone-non-occupée' until the Germans took it over as a counter-measure following the Allied landings in North Africa, in late 1942. On 21 May we arrived at Nozay, near Nantes, which was supposed to be a hospitality centre: schools had been converted into dormitories and field kitchens had been set up to feed the flood of refugees. It was crowded with both Belgian and French civilians, among whom were some British soldiers who had managed, so far, to escape the German net. That night the soldiers invited us to join them at their camp fire while they awaited further orders. We sang songs well-known to us all: 'It's a Long Way to Tipperary', from the First World War and 'We're Going to Hang out Our Washing on the Siegfried Line' of more recent vintage. That evening filled us with hope, a rare commodity just then, and we were much heartened to be told, 'We're going to get your country back for you, however long it takes.' But by the following day the overall picture had changed: the bridges over the River Somme had been destroyed and so our life-line with Belgium had been cut. There was nothing else for it but to go further south still.

On 27 May our column reached Limoges and once more we were billeted in a school. The next and fateful day, 28 May, we drove on, without stopping either in large towns or in villages on the way; it was very plain that those people who recognized us as Belgian were most unfriendly. Some shook their fists at us or shouted insults: it was a shock and we could not imagine what had caused such sudden and extreme hostility. That night we stopped at Cahors and only then did we learn that King Leopold had, that very morning, ordered the Belgian armed forces to cease fighting.

The fact that our country had capitulated came as a dreadful shock; we were incredulous, humiliated, shattered and utterly miserable. To make things worse, we were informed brusquely that there would no longer be any billets available for us; everywhere the French were throwing the Belgians out of their homes. This reaction on the part of our French allies was hard to bear, especially when we remembered that if the French had only managed to hold the Germans at Sedan, there might well have been no need for an Allied capitulation.

In spite of this atmosphere of hostility some of us decided to go into a bistro for some coffee; we were quite exhausted and we hoped to hear some detailed news. Sure enough, the radio was on and the Belgian prime minister was talking. We were deeply moved. When he finished, there came the Belgian national anthem and I am sure that I was not the only one there on the verge of tears. Then M. Reynaud, the French prime minister, spoke. He piled all the blame for the Allied reverses on to our nation and on to King Leopold; as he did so, the people around us made loud and insulting remarks, clearly intended to come to our ears. Our tears of regret quickly turned to tears of rage. It was not until after the war that we learned that, in order to appease his own people, he had to ascribe responsibility for defeat to the Belgians and, especially, to their king.

We were on the point of lashing out bitterly, verbally and otherwise, when some French officers came in and took in the situation; they turned off the radio and apologized for the behaviour of their compatriots. That night the good nuns of a nearby convent offered us shelter; we were profoundly touched.

That day remains one of the most painful of my life.

2

War Work

FOR several more months Cahors was to be our base. A close camar-
aderie had grown up between us all and, although we spent many days
away from our base on varied duties, it was always a relief to report
back and be with our friends again. Our country, our homes and our
families were in more senses than one a long way off; life was now our
duty. We all shared a large dormitory and this had the effect of uniting
us as a family; we lent each other items of clothing and equipment and
exchanged notes at the end of each day. Some days were difficult indeed
and the feeling of mutual support was a source of great strength. There
were, of course, problems; one of these was totally unanticipated,
very unpleasant and very basic: we all needed to be deloused, frequently.
No matter how thorough and effective each treatment, the unpleasant
necessity soon became evident again – and in our tight community we
had to share even this recurrent plague.

The process was quite simple. Items of clothing were baked while
each of us enjoyed a prolonged shower. After this, all body hair had to
be treated with a strong-smelling ointment; we often saw each other, in
Eve's attire, standing very still while the commandant put on her glasses
and with her swabs applied the ointment where it was needed. As I said,
we had become a family, and so we had little or no modesty about such
necessities.

From Cahors we were sent out daily in twos and threes to help care
for the thousands of young men who, having managed to escape from
Belgium, were now housed in our army recruitment and training camps,
waiting for they knew not what. These young men now found themselves marooned in southern France, in the most primitive accommodation and lacking almost all the amenities of life. Together with Agnes

Hendrickx, who was destined to be such a help to me in 1942, I was appointed to work from the small town of Auch, in the *département* of Gers. In our camp, as in most such camps, there was a representative of the Red Cross; in some there was also a Belgian army officer who had managed to avoid capture and to make his way to us. The officers did their best to help organize these camps on military lines, despite the many and severe difficulties. Together, we all did what we could for our young countrymen.

The recruits were a pathetic sight. Either under instruction or out of fear, most of them had left Belgium quickly and without being able to collect very much in the way of clothing and other essentials. Some of them were very young indeed; many of them possessed clothing which was, by now, very tatty; there were grave shortages of items such as underwear and towels. Often the rations were wholly inadequate: the food which should, in theory, have been supplied, sometimes failed to arrive. Our host country was itself severely disorganized. Morale, as might be imagined, was low.

The crude sanitation and the general malnutrition caused some grave problems; dysentery was rife and everyone had lice – which, as I have explained, we members of the Ambulance Corps inevitably caught. We were often sent hundreds of miles, driving lorries, to pick up food from supplies earmarked for Belgian use. Sometimes, after just such a long journey, there would be no supplies available and our trip would have been in vain. One day, however, the arrangements were successful and I picked up an ample supply: my lorry was loaded to the roof with enormous blocks of cheese and many thousands of eggs. This lot, I thought, would be eagerly awaited, so I set off happily for 'base'. Alas, it was not to be. Driving through the mountains somewhere near Clermont-Ferrand, I collided with a car at a sharp bend in the road; I hardly needed to look to assure myself that the greater part of my eggs were thoroughly smashed. With help I got the lorry moving and limped slowly back to camp. It was a hot day in July and by the time I arrived at base the stench of those eggs was quite dreadful. I spent two awful days thoroughly scrubbing the inside of the lorry while mechanics put right the physical damage, but even so I was afflicted for several days afterwards with the occasional whiff. For a long time there was no competition among the crews to ride in that particular vehicle.

Eventually, orders arrived: all young men had to return to German-occupied Belgium. Cattle-trucks, the notorious *'Chevaux 8, Hommes 40'*, were provided, their floors covered with straw. Trainloads of men were sent off, usually without enough food and water and with only the crudest attempt at sanitation; such was the failure of organization. We members of the Corps drove them to the railway station, assisted in getting them settled in (often having to supply necessary first-aid before they set off on a journey which would take a couple of days or more) and generally tried to provide whatever facilities we could muster. In the end all camps were empty and then we, too, were told to prepare to return to Belgium.

There were some, however, including my sister, who were to remain in France for a little longer: her job was now to organize the return home of the many thousands of Belgian civilians who had fled to southern France hoping to escape the Germans. After the capitulation there seemed nothing else for them to do but return to Belgium, but many of them had no means of transport. Even those with cars were in difficulty: petrol was in short supply and so was money. The Germans, we knew, were checking very carefully all returning Belgian citizens; some people suspected, and often rightly, that it would be better not to attract the attention of German officialdom. Some others, who had been politically active, were in any case refused permission to go back. However, the Red Cross did organize the return of many groups, by train and by road.

Defeat is a bitter pill to swallow. Despite Belgium's surrender I still hoped to be able to go on fighting somehow, and obviously this would mean finding some way to get to England. I decided that I must ask the head of my unit to release me and asked for an interview. Madeleine de Lantsheere, our commanding officer, looked at me and waited.

I said, 'I think I've done about all I can. Certainly I don't want to go back and work in a country occupied by the enemy – I want to go to England. There must be something I can do to help our friends fight on. So I want you to release me!'

She looked at me – sympathetically, I thought – but she was very definite. 'I know how you feel. There must be many other people who feel the same way. But we must follow the example of the King: we must go back home and do what we can there. I'm afraid your duty is to the Motor Corps. Believe me, we need your services, and the services of everybody like you.'

So that was that. She was right, of course – in a way; but I was disappointed.

By 10 September there was nothing more to be done and the various sections of the Motor Corps reassembled; we started to drive home as an organized column. Somewhere on the way we parked one evening in

26

the central square of a little French town and found there a large group of Jewish fellow-countrymen who were heading in the opposite direction: they were trying to reach Spain.

When we spoke to them, they conveyed acute anxiety and unhappiness about the German occupation of Belgium. We did not fully understand and found it difficult to believe what they were saying: at that time the news of the harassment suffered by Jews in Germany had not leaked into the outside world. We had heard vague rumours, of course, but could attach little credence to them: civilized people in the twentieth century, we thought, could not act in such a way. They, however, had their own sources of information; they knew of the persecution and of the transports to camps. But they did not, I think, even then suspect that the Final Solution meant mass murder, genocide. They had already come to despair of convincing the outside world even of the comparatively minor atrocities which were already taking place. 'Minor' by later standards, that is. So we said our adieux and the columns separated: we headed back to enemy-occupied Belgium, while they pressed on south and west to an uncertain future. I sometimes wondered, in the days that followed, what became of them.

When we passed over the demarcation line between unoccupied and occupied France, we had our first encounter with the German army. Somewhere we stopped for the night in a small town and found that a Panzer division was already quartered there. The men were smart and obviously disciplined; they were well-organized, in strong contrast to the French units now waiting their turn to be told where to report for their new lives as prisoners of war. The German officers, noting that some of the vehicles of our ambulance unit were driven by good-looking young women, came over and attempted to fraternize. We refused to shake hands or to enter into conversation; we insisted on total formality in what little was said and tried to disappear from their notice as rapidly as we could.

However, the Germans, always thorough and perhaps, by now, a little nettled by our obvious hostility, insisted on examining all our identification cards. They spotted immediately that the photograph on the card belonging to Eliane de Spoelberch had been tampered with. In fact she had changed the photo herself, believing that the official photo did not do her justice. She was taken at once to the local prison at Niort, to be held there pending investigation. The poor girl who, like almost all of us, had come from a very sheltered background, had to spend several weeks with thieves, prostitutes and even murderers – and in the insalubrious surroundings of a French gaol. Madame Lippens, a very high-ranking Red Cross official, went with Fee d'Alcantara to try to get her released. Fee had been born Princess Windishgraetz, the name of an old and respected Austrian family, and spoke perfect German. She was told that she must take up the matter with the Hauptmann, who was installed with his staff in a nearby château. When the two women got there, they found a lot of young men playing football clad only in their underwear. The Hauptmann was among the players: he walked up to the women, who were startled to find that he was wearing only a transparent slip and his monocle. He gave the Hitler salute to our perfectly-dressed, large lady commander, who stood there unflinching. If the encounter achieved nothing else, at least it illustrated correct behaviour.*

Finally we crossed the frontier into Belgium and were home from our wanderings; it had seemed an age. We had much to catch up on. King Leopold now considered himself a prisoner of war and lived in self-imposed captivity, mostly in his castle at Laeken. Prime Minister Pierlot and his government were in France. There had been some discussion within the Pierlot government about going to London and, indeed, there were deep divisions among ministers about what action to take. The Belgian Ambassador in London, Baron Cartier de Marchiennes, urged the Belgian government to go to England right away.

At Bordeaux on 18 June 1940, Prime Minister Pierlot took the decision to send the Minister of Colonies, Mr De Vleeschauwer, to London to take charge of the Belgian interests in the Congo. He was to be the Administrator of the Belgian Congo, Ruanda and Urundi. Mr De Vleeschauwer had, from the start, wanted to go to England to continue the fight and, on 25 June, he told the British Ambassador that he was determined to afford the utmost assistance to the British cause.

In June 1940 the Minister of Finance, Mr Camille Gutt, joined him in London. But the rest of the government, when in Bordeaux and then in Vichy, were still uncertain what to do and there was talk of going to the United States. Mr Pierlot, with Paul Henri Spaak and several other ministers, eventually left in August for Spain, where they were virtually prisoners of the Spanish government. Despite diplomatic intervention by Britain and Belgium, the Spaniards refused to release their detainees. Eventually Pierlot and Spaak were smuggled out of Spain into Portugal and thence to England.** They arrived in London on 22 October 1940.

---

*Some two months later, Eliane was released and rejoined us in Belgium.
**cf. *Le Roi Leopold III de Belgique*, p.127 (see Bibliography).

The Germans had some of their best troops in our country and were at pains to behave correctly; the French, our neighbours and allies, were not friendly to the Belgians and *petits Belges*, which had been a term of endearment in World War I, was now used as a term of derision. For ourselves, we were very disappointed that the RAF had not been able to do more to protect us when the German aircraft roamed the skies at will. Nevertheless, in the end commonsense prevailed and we realized that even if the performance of our allies had been disappointing, it was the Germans who remained the enemies of us all. They had invaded our country without any provocation whatsoever – like the leopard, they had not changed their spots. Once again, my father's earlier prophecies had been proved true. Many thousands of Belgians, including (as I later found) my brother John, were in prisoner-of-war camps. It was significant, however, that the Germans had released and sent home all Flemish, non-regular army personnel: perhaps they thought that these men might, before long, be won over as useful allies. If they did think that, they were soon to be disappointed.

While still in France I had had some news of my family. My father, as the Mayor of Jurbise, would not leave until forced to do so, when one day French troops arrived with instructions to hold a line running directly across our grounds. Father was not allowed to collect the most elementary necessities – a change of clothing and washing things – and even as he was leaving, he saw the French soldiers already beginning to loot the château. War is war, he thought, philosophically, and set off on foot, flanked by the village priest and the local policeman. These three were followed by most of the people of Jurbise, including the nuns of a nearby convent, who found it difficult to walk far in their wooden clogs. The group managed to stay together and in the next ten days they walked no less than 300 kilometres. Everybody ate as best they could – often sharing what food they found in abandoned houses. In the end, the advancing Germans caught up with them and, after a brief conference, offered to return them to Jurbise, riding in Wehrmacht vehicles. Very sensibly, the villagers accepted this offer.

My mother and my four younger brothers, I heard, had left Belgium; the two older boys had been ordered to report to the Belgian Army Recruitment Centre, the CRAB, at one of their camps in France. They all set off, together with some friends and relatives, in two cars; one was driven by my brother Alain (now a competent driver – thanks, perhaps, to our illicit operations of earlier years) and the other by Xavier, who had had practically no driving experience. In due course the whole party

29

arrived safely at a village in unoccupied France. There they settled for a time to await developments; some weeks later they returned home.

By October 1940 the Motor Corps was functioning smoothly again, though on a reduced scale: petrol was very short and in addition to this, our ranks were depleted by the necessity to help out with the functioning of the inadequate ambulance services of several cities. Nevertheless, it was essential that we kept the Corps in operation and fully trained; one day Belgium would be liberated and we imagined that this would necessarily entail very heavy fighting. The Germans, we knew, did not easily yield what they had once won. Undoubtedly there would be work for us, so we toiled on. Usually we worked for two full days a week but there were times when we were very busy and had to work on the other days as well.

That work sometimes led us into strange situations. One day my companion and I had to bring down an elderly man from the fourth floor of an old house. There was no lift; the stairs were very narrow, very steep and badly lit; our patient was wrapped only in a sheet. It was not possible to use a stretcher; the patient was too ill to be brought down in a chair. Accordingly, we held the man in the sheet and inched our way down step by step. I could see the strain written in my friend's face and her clenched teeth; no doubt she could read the same strain in me. It was touch and go whether we would get him safely down without all three of us falling in a tangled heap, but our patient evidently noticed nothing and finally we did reach the ground floor. There we paused to let our breathing get back to normal; then we exchanged mutually congratulatory glances and got our patient the last few yards to the ambulance. We drove off in an absolute daze of achievement.

One day, my sister Bee was driving an inert and sedated patient who suddenly startled her by shouting, 'Red fingernails, Red Cross. Everything I see is red. I must be going mad!' It was a disquieting moment for a young woman, unaccompanied and driving along a deserted country road. Another time, one of our number was driving a patient to hospital in a car; he had been, she believed, heavily sedated. She was concentrating on a difficult road when she felt two hands from behind meeting around her neck: the patient had gone completely berserk. Fortunately, she was able to bring her car to a screeching stop and to attract the attention of passers-by, who came to her assistance. The patient was overpowered and tied down firmly with a convenient length of rope, and the journey continued – with a couple of volunteers to keep an eye on things. When the episode was later recounted in the canteen, the drama somehow became transmuted into comedy; yet it had been a dangerous moment and we all learned from it.

Occasionally we were sent into France to collect serious cases; such trips were always valuable as we managed to pick up odd items of news. On several occasions I went to Paris, which was, of course, in the occupied zone. People there complained to me that food was scarce, yet many restaurants – particularly the dearest – were open and obviously thriving; theatres of all kinds were playing to packed houses. French women were still, as ever, fashion-conscious, but as there were not enough clothing coupons for them to indulge their fancy freely in dresses, their flair expressed itself mainly in very decorative hats. In fact, to a casual observer the only difference between prewar Paris and 1940 Paris was the abundance of German uniforms: all branches of the Wehrmacht and of its numerous auxiliary formations dominated the street scene. The atmosphere seemed to be relaxed: at that time, certainly, the Germans were taking great pains to behave correctly and it was noticeable, to my Belgian eyes, that many of the conquerors had acquired companions from among the local young ladies. It seemed obvious that the Germans were more accepted here than they were in Brussels, but that is purely a subjective impression.

In October of 1940 I managed to get some leave and departed to spend a few days with the family at Jurbise. It was then I heard that in the first days of the war my parents had been told, inaccurately, happily, that my eldest brother John had been killed. Details had been lacking, but it was several days before they were overjoyed to be informed officially that he was very much alive and well. To this day I do not know how the report came about but, as I have said earlier, rumours and counter-rumours abounded and created great anxiety and often distress. While at Jurbise I found that a number of Italian officers of the Regia Aeronautica – the Italian air force – had been billeted at the château. Some months earlier, when it was obvious that France was about to collapse, Mussolini had declared war on the Allies: the jackal wanted a share of the expected carcase. There have been few historical miscalculations on so grand a scale, one which brought untold suffering and loss to the Italian people. Now the Italian dictator was clamouring for his aircrews to have their share in what he mistakenly considered to be the decisive assault on the British Isles.

'Our' airmen were stationed at an airfield only five miles away and all the large houses in the neighbourhood of Jurbise had been thus requisitioned. One of our visitors was Tenente Vittorio Mussolini, the nephew

31

of the Duce himself; another was Capitano Rapetti, former editor of the *Popolo d'Italia*, the authoritative daily paper and semi-official mouth-piece of the Fascist regime. The other officers were all regulars and there were several batmen. 'Vito' Mussolini had the same square jaw and lack of hair as his uncle, was just as arrogant and was also addicted to striking heroic poses – chin raised and jutting forward. It was wholly obvious that his family connection conveyed more status than his lowly rank: Captain Rapetti was clearly little more than an aide to his official junior. The Germans, who might have had their private reservations about the fighting qualities of their Italian allies, showed overt respect for the Tenente and treated him as an honoured guest.

Even the local people looked upon the Italians with a mixture of sour amusement and contempt. These feelings found expression in an endless stream of jokes, passed from one of us to another, after precautionary glances over each shoulder to ensure that none of the latter-day Romans was in earshot. On such story – apocryphal, of course – goes as follows: Mussolini himself came to Belgium to visit an airfield and visit his brave aviators. One morning there was a most impressive parade, following which eighteen crews ran to their bombers and roared away to attack England.

'At what time do you expect them back?' the Duce asked the commanding officer.

'About midday,' was the answer.

But by eleven o'clock the bombers were returning. Benito counted them passing overhead and remarked. 'Only eighteen went out but nineteen have returned. Look, there's an extra one at the rear.'

'Oh, him,' said the Italian CO. 'That's the RAF plane which chased them all home.'

My family, of course, lived separately from the Italians: fortunately the house was big enough for them to have their own entrance and rooms and so we fraternized very little. But sometimes, in the evening, Italian officers would knock at our door and ask if they could join us in listening to the BBC; such listening was, of course, strictly forbidden to victors and vanquished alike, yet we made a practice of tuning in every evening for the satisfaction of hearing the voice of a free and defiant ally, giving out news infinitely more trustworthy than that churned out by the German and Italian propaganda machines. The Italians usually wanted to listen on days when they had been on a raid over England to find out what had really happened. On one occasion an Italian told us that having crossed the English coast he had quickly dropped his bombs

32

and turned back while he and his crew were still unscathed. On another occasion the Italian formation had somehow managed to get themselves thoroughly lost – only to find out that they were over Reims, miles away from their intended course. There were times when they would brag of their successes: it seemed as if they were trying to outbid each other in boasting. I could hardly take them seriously: they were so obviously overgrown children play-acting in ornate uniforms, but my father used to become intensely irritated. He would manage to contain himself for a time, but would eventually mention Caporetto, a name of shame to the Italian armed forces. That was when the whole Italian army broke and fled before the Austrians in 1917, a day of ignominy and one which all Italians tried hard to forget. When the conversation reached such a point, the Italians present would excuse themselves and leave, some of them clearly restraining anger only with an effort.

I vividly remember Christmas 1940. We, the family, were sitting in silence, listening to King George speaking from London. Several Italian officers came into the room and listened with us. After the speech came the British national anthem; my mother, herself half-English, rose to her feet and the family followed her example. To our amazement, the Italians also stood. Later they left quietly and we had no means of knowing what effect the speech had had on their outlook.

These officers were incredibly indiscreet: they not only showed us aerial photographs of our château and of others nearby (including beautiful Beloeil), but also of the airfields which they were using – Melsbroeck and Chièvres, I remember, and there may have been more. Of course we all, Belgians and Italians alike, had to be careful about what was said in front of Tenente Mussolini, but when he was absent Captain Rapetti, for one, would discuss the war very frankly. We asked him whether he was ashamed to bomb civilian targets but he told us that he was an Italian officer and as such he had to obey orders.

One day, I remember, my father said, 'You must realize that in the end the Germans will lose the war. The longer the war lasts, the more surely will the Germans lose.'

'Not so,' he replied. 'With our courage and German *matériel* we shall conquer the world.'

He seemed to believe it. I would have liked, some years later, to have reminded him of his confidence that day but, as will be seen, the war took us in different directions.

One morning all the Italian officers seemed very pleased about something or other. We did not ask any questions: knowing our men, we simply waited for them to tell us. Indeed, that same evening they did so, unable to contain their joy and pride any longer. They had just received some new aircraft, and they were so proud of them that they actually invited us to go and inspect them on the following day. I pointed out that the airfield was so vast that we would not know where to go, and one of them then drew me a detailed sketch to show where their new aircraft were parked. Incredible! If the machines were as new as all that, then obviously we must go and inspect them, remembering as much of the detail as possible. Already we knew that all such intelligence was valuable and that there would soon be ways of getting it across the water to England.

The new machines, it turned out, were Cant 1007 bis. Scattered about the airfield were many other aircraft – a mixture of Fiat CR42 biplane fighters and Savoia-Marchetti three-engined bombers. Nothing very new or memorable about those. The Cants, when we came to them, were apparently the latest weapons in the Axis armoury and between us we took pains to memorize all the facts and figures so proudly set out for us. The 1007 bis was a three-engined bomber, the engines were each of 1000 hp and the aircraft carried a crew of five. It had a bomb load of 4500 lb and an armament of four machine-guns. It cruised at 240 mph, with a maximum speed of almost 300 mph. (Despite ourselves we found all this impressive.) The ceiling was 21,000 feet and the range was 1500 miles. As I said, between us we ensured that all these figures were retained; however meaningless they might be to us, we knew that all such information would be gladly received elsewhere – once we found ways of passing it on. Still, however excellent the aircraft, we comforted ourselves with the thought that they were manned by Italians; already they had demonstrated that for many of them the war was quite undeserving of whatever funds of heroism they could raise. Over England, we thought, this new super-bomber would undoubtedly be badly mauled, and if proof were needed of the validity of our suspicions, it was amply provided some months later when all the Italians and their varied aircraft were moved to the Mediterranean area where, at that time, the opposition was not so intense.

So ended my first venture into intelligence gathering but there were to be many more. Up to the time that the Italians left I made a point of paying visits to Jurbise as often as I could; there I would collect from my parents and from one or two reliable local contacts as much information as they had been able to acquire. In this we were assisted by the total lack of security shown by the Italians: officers and men alike, they were remarkably indiscreet. The batmen and the various tradesmen working with the aircraft all talked freely to the local people. Most of them, very sensibly and like the aircrews themselves, intensely disliked being at war and emphasized to us that Italy was not at war with Belgium, and that they hated the Germans. The Tedeschi, in their turn, made no secret of their low opinion of their Latin allies. One of the batmen quartered at Jurbise, incidentally, was the champion roller-skater of Italy and wanted only to be back in familiar surroundings. He did not hide his loathing of the occasional German visitor to the château; to their faces he was deferential enough but behind their backs he would make gestures of contempt, even pretending to shoot them. Then he would wink at us.

We noticed that the Italians, talking to each other, made frequent use of code words. One such was 'vermouth' and another was 'cinzano'. We racked our brains and argued with each other about what these words might mean. There were clues: the word 'vermouth', heard early in the day, was inevitably followed by great agitation and we deduced that it meant a raid over England; the other word, 'cinzano', we found out eventually, meant some kind of exercise. We had confirmation one evening. We were settling down to listen to a BBC bulletin when Captain Rapetti knocked at our door and asked, 'May I please listen to the English broadcast? Their information is generally correct.' He sat down in a corner and we heard – 'A raid, in which the Italian air force was involved, has taken place in the south of England. Several Italian planes were destroyed and the rest scattered like sparrows. Their bombs were jettisoned over open country or even over the sea, as they turned and ran for safety.'

That very morning there had been much talk of 'vermouth' and the usual worried faces. We came to know that the Italian aircraft were used mainly to bait the RAF into intercepting them; then, when the British were thought to be refuelling, the German aircraft would go in with considerably more determination.

It was because of the Italian presence at Jurbise that, in October 1940, I first became involved with the emergent Belgian underground. I mentioned to an old friend, Christian Lancksweert, that Italian officers were billeted at the château and he asked me to collect as much information as I could. Christian, I knew, had been an officer in the Belgian regular army and he had somehow avoided being imprisoned. I knew very little, of course, about military matters, but thenceforth an agent known to me as K1 used to visit me from time to time and I was trained in various useful arts: how to recognize the silhouettes of aircraft, both Allied and enemy; how to draw a target map with tolerable accuracy; and how to note down the different unit markings on all types of enemy vehicles. I was also asked to find out where the petrol and munition dumps were and, if possible, discover the thickness of the concrete that protected them. There was great satisfaction in knowing that even now I might be of use to my subjugated country.

When I thought how easily young children recognized cars and air-craft after only the merest glance, I felt very stupid as I pored over my chart of silhouettes. The Ju 87 Stuka was, of course, both familiar and unmistakable; by October of 1940 I had seen them much too often – both in action and then later, after the surrender, flying to and from local aerodromes. They were ugly, slow and very noisy, and the noise increased as they rolled over and dived. The Me 109, the standard German fighter of the time, was sleek and had squared-off wing tips; the Me 110 had two engines and twin rudders, and was used as a fighter-bomber. I had seen Me 110s attacking refugee columns and had had to witness the horrifying results of such attacks. The twin-engined, stubby He 111 bomber had distinctive wings, seen in plan form, and a glassed-in nose; the Dornier 17s were sleeker and had twin fins. Soon I could recognize them all with ease and certainty, whether in flight or on the ground; I made a point of counting any I saw on the ground so that I could report both type and number. I also learned how to recognize the various German uniforms which I saw as I drove about the country: Luftwaffe, Kriegsmarine, Army and SS.

As I was only intermittently at Jurbise, I enlisted my brother Xavier to help out during my absences. He was to keep in touch with M. Tibonne, who lived near the Chièvres airbase and from that position of vantage supplied us with information. He was a radio engineer, and he travelled widely over the immediate area, repairing people's radios. He was a good technician, which was to be very useful to us later, and was wholly reliable. Xavier would cycle across to meet him and collect any information, written very carefully on cigarette paper. This would be hidden in the handlebar of the bike. If the information was urgent, he would even bring it to me in Brussels. One day, returning from Chièvres along the main road, he was stopped by the Feldgendarmerie, the German military police, for a spot check. He was searched fairly thoroughly but the Germans did not think of looking inside his handlebars; nor did his demeanour betray any sign of fear or guilt. After a 'mauvais quart d'heure' he was allowed to go, but the experience had been a warning and thenceforth he always took paths across the fields, avoiding the roads.

So, gradually, I was drawn into a new activity; my life was entering a dangerous world, one of which I had never dreamed. I was quite unprepared for it, of course, and I had to learn as I went along – as did so many others. We began to function as spies in our own country, now under the heel of German occupation.

3

Belgium under the Heel

AT this point it might be timely to give a brief account of events at home while we of the Motor Corps were busy elsewhere – and of the gradual unfolding of events through the winter of 1940 into 1941 and 1942.

Immediately following the surrender, the streets of every town and village in our land took on a new aspect. Swastika flags hung everywhere and flew from all public buildings. True, these flags often disappeared mysteriously during the night but there was evidently an endless supply somewhere and any missing flag was immediately replaced. The gesture, however, was satisfying – even if the municipality was heavily fined for the 'crime'. It was striking to what extent German uniforms abounded everywhere – army mainly, with Luftwaffe a close second. In coastal areas the Kriegsmarine was conspicuous, and everywhere one saw Organization Todt brown uniforms. Aerodromes were enlarged or built from scratch, and coastal defences were built up so as to deny the Allies any chance of returning to the mainland from which they had been expelled. Many of the hostile uniforms were worn by women: Luftwaffe auxiliaries or Nazi Party welfare workers.

We were soon told that whereas the Netherlands was to have a civilian administration under the dreadful Reichskommisar Seyss-Inquart (who was to be executed at Nuremberg in 1946), Belgium was to remain under military rule. Our overlord was General von Falkenhausen; this was, initially at least, ominous, for he was the nephew of the officer of the same name who had administered Belgium from April 1917 to the end of that war. In those twenty months he ordered the execution of some 200 Belgian citizens, and flogged or deported many thousands more. This new von Falkenhausen was a complex character. Although we had no means of knowing it, he was privately anti-Nazi and during his term of office he did much to frustrate the more extreme demands of the SS. Even before the July 1944 plot he had already been consigned to a concentration camp. However, we did not see that side of him; to us he was a figure of authority, scrupulously just, tough but fair. On many occasions he yielded to pleas and reprieved men and women who would otherwise have ended up in Dachau or Sachsenhausen or one of the other camps. He spoke fluent English and was an interested student of the English way of life. He was, I suppose, a typical product of the best German military tradition. Incidentally, he was earmarked to be military commander in Britain – when the Germans got there! His right-hand man was a General Reeder and together they administered our country rigidly.

The greatest opponent of von Falkenhausen's methods, although we were unaware of it at the time, was Otto Kammerstein, head of the Gestapo in Belgium. He was an almost unknown man, appearing in public very seldom and never mentioned in the press. Yet he was a man who wielded great power. In spite of the care he took not to be recognized, he was shot dead in the latter part of the war by relatives of one of his victims.

At the start of the occupation the Germans pegged the currency at 10 francs to 1 Reichsmark – as against the original value which varied between 3 and 6. Before the end of July this value had been changed to 12.5 francs to 1 RM – and many of their occupation notes, we were interested to see, had been printed as early as May 1935. Truly, the Germans had laid their plans well in advance. With all this printed money and the extortionate rate of exchange, Belgium was soon suffering from roaring inflation. Shop windows emptied as the Wehrmacht personnel sent frequent parcels to their relatives at home. To make things worse, the Germans began to requisition all manner of things and in large quantities: cattle, food, pigs, coal, rolling-stock, lorries, textiles, leather and hides, horses. Most petrol stocks were confiscated, but the effects of this were somewhat alleviated by the readiness of German soldiers to sell black-market petrol at inflated prices.

The whole structure of life was altered. The Third Reich took charge of law and order – and often allocated to these twin concepts meanings hitherto unimagined. The whole economy of the country, industrial and agricultural, was redesigned to meet the demands of the occupying power. Even as the German armies crossed our frontiers on 10 May 1940, the first decrees – long prepared – were being posted up. But local government still functioned in more or less normal fashion.

Schools were re-opened; the police went about their work; the various ancillary functions of the state – communications, medical services, power and the like – functioned almost as normal, but subject, where necessary, to the final control of the Germans. There was, however, no central Belgian government: the elected and legal government, headed by Prime Minister Pierlot, had reached London; King Leopold himself had retired to his castle at Laeken and announced that he considered himself as much a prisoner of war as were many of his soldiers.

Food rationing was quickly introduced. The amounts were small enough, but even so there were often times when supplies in the shops were inadequate to honour the coupons. Those coupons, by the way, were forged with relative ease, so the colour and design had to be changed frequently. By the winter of 1940 the rations were as follows (all amounts are weekly, and are given in the nearest avoirdupois equivalent to the metrical quantity):

Bread: 3 lb 1 oz (the bread was black and sticky, and impossible to slice; it contained a legally fixed admixture of 'edible bark')
Butter: 1½ oz
Margarine: 1¾ oz
Potatoes: 6 lbs 8 oz
Milk (skimmed): 7 pt
Meat: 10½ oz (including 20% bone)
Rice: 1½ oz
Sugar: ½ oz
Coffee (ersatz): 2¼ oz
Syrup: 1½ oz
Vegetables (dried): 1½ oz
Oil: ½ oz

Those people living in coastal areas might well, illicitly or otherwise, be able to add a little fish. There was a black market operating but prices were very high and small savings were soon spent. A labourer – not highly paid – with several children could not afford to buy food over and above the ration, and people's health was soon affected. It was estimated that within the first twelve months the average person lost more than a stone in weight. There were, of course, some beneficial side-effects: my dear mother, who had become with the years a rather plump lady, recovered her girlish figure, despite having borne seven children.

Great efforts were made to grow more food. Every flowerbed was given over to potatoes or cabbage; lawns were dug over; not an inch of land was wasted. Anyone who could keep a few chickens or a sheep or a pig did so, although this was, strictly speaking, illegal. We often went off into the countryside, foraging. I remember on one occasion using my official *Passierschein* (permit to travel), issued to me as a member of the Motor Corps, to bring back a suitcase full of pieces of lamb to my grandparents in Brussels. The lamb had been killed secretly at Jurbise and the family were worried about our grandparents in Brussels, so we just had to risk the checks at the railway stations. At the stations patrols of German soldiers made occasional searches of passengers' luggage, looking for just such smuggled food. If they found any, the food would be confiscated and the bearer would be prosecuted. It was often very sad to see quite small children stopped and their supplies taken from them; it was an even sadder sight to see such children openly begging for food in the street – unimaginable in prewar Belgium.

During November of 1941, 100,000 people in the province of Limburg had no potatoes at all; in Brussels itself there was often no bread for weeks on end. The complete ration scale, when fully honoured, amounted to at most 1000 calories a day; a normal adult needs 2500 calories a day to maintain good health – and more than that if he is a manual worker. At one time over 7000 Belgians were awaiting trial for obtaining food over and above the ration.

To ameliorate the position, several new organizations came into being. There was the Secours d'Hiver, modelled on the Nazi 'Winterhilfe'; this organization was not popular because of the German connection, but it did good work in providing food and coal for the poorest of our people. Indeed, the Germans did not want a national famine; not only would the loss in the propaganda war have been considerable, but they did not want to risk a general insurrection.

The Red Cross expanded its role and organized canteens where the needy could get regular meals; in this they were assisted by the Red Cross Societies of other nations not involved in the war. Now and then, for example, a consignment of sardines would reach us from Portugal and in the winter of 1942 there was a near miracle: a few fishermen allowed out to fish (within sight of our coastline) brought in 40,000 tons of herrings. The Oeuvre National de l'Enfance – a charity devoted solely to the needs of children – was giving effective help and in early 1941 the Princesse de Ligne started a string of food canteens called Foyer Leopold III; these helped primarily children in the poorest and worst-hit districts, mainly in the towns.

41

On days when I was not working for the Motor Corps, I helped to run one of these canteens in Brussels. This canteen was in a large hall in a western suburb called Anderlecht. In this hall, with fairly adequate heating, was a series of large tables each accommodating between twelve and sixteen children sitting on wooden benches. The food was mainly provided by the Service de Ravitaillement, but this would have been less than adequate without the funds provided by Princesse de Ligne which allowed the different sectors to buy some extra rations from the official suppliers. The Red Cross also contributed whenever possible. But the task was difficult. There were 1500 people who were registered for the Anderlecht canteen, although on any given day some did not turn up, and new ones appeared without being on the register.

We recorded that in the first five months of 1941 no fewer than 201,207 people came for a midday meal. It consisted of a little slice of meat some days – sausages were more frequent – vegetables – too often cabbage – and potatoes (one per person), turnips or parsnips. Fruit was very scarce, except in the apple season, as it was only very occasionally that supplies of oranges, tangerines or bananas arrived from a country with a warmer climate. Puddings were also rarely on the menu because of the sugar shortage, but were a source of great pleasure when they did appear. Cheese was sometimes available, but only a very small slice. Milk was provided for the children and the elderly. This food was distributed by local volunteers who would organize events to put a little more money in the kitty and provide a little extra whenever possible. I helped to distribute the food but also worked in the office, doing accounts, checking supplies, monitoring the numbers and the distribution.

We had a nurse attached to the organization and she would look out for cases of severe malnutrition and for tuberculosis, which had been nearly eradicated before the war but which was rapidly coming back. A few children were lucky in that we were able to send them to a sanatorium in Switzerland where the Red Cross looked after them. In spite of all our efforts we could only provide meagre rations and it was heartbreaking to see children looking up hungrily, eager for an extra potato. They never asked – they were too well trained to do that – but as their eyes followed the dishes, their need was all too evident.

It is, perhaps, difficult for anyone who has not known prolonged and fierce hunger to realize the extent of the food problem in Belgium at its most acute during the early years of World War II. In Britain there was, of course, a tight rationing system and a black market but, as I found out later, the rations were on a much more generous basis and real hunger was always avoidable; in Britain certain foods – bread, for example – were never rationed in the war years and the health of the nation actually improved during that time. In any case, I do believe that food had always meant more to the Belgians than to the British; in this respect, Belgium can (almost) be compared to France. There was a saying –

> La France se divide en trois parts:
> L'amour, l'alimentation et l'art.
> Mais ni la peinture, et ni la passion
> Sont plus important que l'alimentation.

Not only food was scarce: very soon after the occupation began, such necessities as shoes, cycle tyres and babies' clothing became very scarce indeed. The Germans tried to put the blame for this on the British blockade, but we all knew that any and every shortage was directly due to official and large-scale German looting.

By the end of 1942 our various desperate measures had prevailed and the food situation had improved; in the later years of the war food was actually being stored against some future shortage. When Brussels was liberated by the Guards Armoured Division in September 1944, food appeared from everywhere, to the amazement of the British troops. The population wanted to make it a great day – and so they did. The festive spirit was assisted in Brussels that day by the large supply of champagne which the Germans had stored in the cellars of the Palais de Justice. Before leaving, the Germans had tried to burn their documents in the building but the champagne had, mercifully, escaped the destruction.

Of course, everyone over the age of thirty remembered the earlier German occupation and with very little effort they now dropped into the accustomed patterns of behaviour – even of resistance, passive or otherwise. Initially the Belgians were quite bewildered by the suddenness and completeness of the débâcle. The war had not followed the pattern of World War I; with the government out of the country there was a political void, and this time the whole country was occupied – as well as most of the European mainland. To increase the confusion, the Germans, who in the First World War had created a great terror, this time did their best to give the impression of behaving correctly. In what daily contacts we had with them they were clearly under orders to be polite, and this impressed the Belgians. So there arose a confused situation: a limited movement towards collaboration, on the one hand, and on the other many-sided resistance to the occupying power. Two circumstances, however, played their part in clarifying our thinking.

The first was the Battle of Britain. We had begun to doubt whether any nation was strong enough or resolute enough to stand up to these new Germans, and when the nightly BBC bulletins told us of the progress of the battle we rejoiced at the successes of the RAF. When, finally, it became clear that Germany was not able to invade Britain, we began to find new hope. Churchill's voice was always a tonic.

Then, in the autumn of 1940, German politeness and correctness cracked and we saw the true face of oppression. Two impending events acquired renewed significance: Armistice Day on 11 November and the King's birthday, a few days later. Belgians prepared to celebrate both days appropriately. Such celebrations would, of course, include an element of national defiance, whatever the occasion ostensibly being remembered. Perhaps someone among the pro-Germans tipped off the occupying power; perhaps the Germans, uncharacteristically, indulged in unwonted forethought. At any rate, an edict was promulgated: Armistice Day was not to be openly celebrated. All gatherings and processions were banned, as were any special church services on the day; all shops and offices were to remain open and everyone was to report for work as usual. We were in no doubt what would happen to offenders: deportations to the Reich for compulsory labour were already under way. That 11 November, nevertheless, the threats went unheeded. Many people marched to the Tomb of the Unknown Warrior to show their determination to remember the past and to demonstrate national unity; the German army, deployed in all streets leading to the Tomb, met the demonstrators and dispersed them, using considerable violence. Yet, despite this attempt to terrorize them, the people of Brussels made their feelings known again, on 15 November, the King's birthday, when there was a mass in the cathedral of St Gudule. At the close of the Te Deum the congregation sang the Brabanconne, and the soft organ playing afterwards could be recognized as the British national anthem. The people finally dispersed, under furious German disapproval, with shouts of 'Long live the King'. In a futile attempt to ensure there would be no recurrence of so defiant a gesture, the authorities arrested some 700 people in Brussels during the next few days. Most were fined and released; a few, who persisted in their German defiance, even in a German-dominated court, received varying terms of imprisonment.

The demonstrations did not, of course, stop. To emphasize their displeasure the Germans imposed a curfew; this acted as a brake on both private and public life and immediately became a major nuisance. We

44

members of the Motor Corps, however, could use our official *Ausweis*, a form of *laissez-passer*, to justify our presence on the streets at any time, pleading duty. In case the curfew alone was not sufficient to enforce the lesson, the food rations of fats and meat were reduced for a time.

In the years before the war Belgium had suffered from high unemployment, and even in August 1940 half a million people were without work. German National Socialism was supposed to eradicate unemployment, and a programme of road building, sewer repair and demolition of derelict housing (rebuilding would only take place *after* the war) was started in Belgium. This was designed to give employment to many thousands of men, but the wages were low and strikes punishable by military court.

To take the place of German workers called up to the fighting services, Belgians were persuaded into going to work in Germany – German propaganda was designed to tempt people to do so. The conditions seemed to be fair; length of hours worked and rates of pay, holidays, accommodation, a fixed length of contract and the chance to remit money to their families at a favourable rate of exchange. But, as it was to turn out later, all these fine promises were to be broken. Once the Belgian worker was in Germany, the work was usually more strenuous and the hours longer than the contract stipulated. That contract itself was arbitrarily prolonged and remittances mysteriously delayed: money would be promptly deducted at source, but would be credited irregularly in Belgium. Small wonder that when, infrequently, a worker did manage to get home on leave, he would often 'vanish' – and occasionally try to escape to England. With the whole European coastline, from North Cape to the Pyrenees, in German hands, and no neutral frontiers nearer than Spain or Switzerland, escape was not easy. But fishermen still had to go out – the Germans themselves imposed a quota on their catches – and it was sometimes possible to tranship an unofficial passenger in the dark and from an agreed rendezvous.

The whole tenor of life under occupation was such that initial resentment at defeat was soon intensified by the measures enforced by the occupying power. At first, any attempts to oppose German rule were unco-ordinated and spontaneous – but widespread. The Civil Service exerted a passive resistance, taking at least twice as long as usual over all processes – particularly those to do with meeting German quotas. Magistrates interpreted the law in the light of the situation, where 'criminals' were often, in natural justice, no criminals at all. Universities

45

refused to submit lists of students who might well, they suspected, be taken for forced labour – probably in Germany.

Soon 'razzias' became common: you would realize that both ends of the street in which you were had been blocked by strong forces of heavily armed German soldiers, while patrols would ensure that nobody dived into convenient shops or houses. Everybody would have to show identity papers; anybody thought to be suspicious would be taken away for more detailed questioning – and at best would return after several hours or even a day or two. At worst, a postcard would arrive from Germany, asking for clothing and essential articles.

Many secret underground newspapers appeared – the first was called *Chut* and was published in Brussels on 15 June 1940; within the first six months of the occupation there were at least eighty such newspapers in circulation. They were often run off on small home or office duplicators and had a low print-run. The publishers frequently moved base – whenever it was feared the Germans were getting near to locating them; the copies were passed surreptitiously from hand to hand. They would be stealthily hidden in a shopping basket, carefully unfolded and read in a safe place, and equally carefully refolded and passed on.

By the middle of August 1940 the underground *Libre Belgique* had a print-run of no less than 400,000 and was widely distributed by a network of brave and resourceful couriers. It gave its telegraphic address as the German *Kommandantur* in Brussels, and its editor was, ostensibly, Peter Pan – the name of the well-known statue in the Jardin d'Egmont in Brussels. We were all deeply grateful to the brave men who risked their lives – no less – to produce and distribute it. The paper was, of course, important to us, but it was on the BBC that we really relied.

An anecdote, much told at the time, about the BBC:

Scene: a street in Brussels. It is evening. A German officer stops a passing civilian and asks, politely,
'Excuse me, but do you know the time?'
Civilian, unhelpfully, 'I have no watch.'
A little girl, passing, 'It is just after half-past seven.'
German officer: 'Thank you. But how do you know the time so exactly? I can see you have no watch.'
Little girl, scornfully, 'Can't you see that there is nobody in the street? They have all gone indoors. The BBC news starts at half-past seven.'

The old and trusted newspaper *Le Soir* had been taken over by the Germans and now appeared thanks to the co-operation of a number of collaborators. It was at once dubbed *Le Soir volé* and its circulation dropped dramatically. On 9 November 1943, however, cyclists delivered thousands of copies of a pirated version of *Le Soir*, carrying pro-Ally, anti-German and anti-collaborator articles. Despite frantic enquiries, the perpetrators were never found.

Life became difficult in every respect. At the end of three months of occupation the Germans demanded that all instruction at the university of Brussels should be given in Flemish, a move clearly intended to break national unity and to curry the favour of the Flemish. The council of the university – as many Flemish as Walloons – rejected this demand outright, but in order to be allowed to function at all the university had to make some kind of concessions to the German authorities.

At the beginning of October the Germans demanded that all Jews should be removed from the university and from every kind of governmental or municipal post. This demand was refused outright: according to Article 6 of the Belgian constitution, all Belgians were equal before the law, regardless of race or religion; but all Jews were compelled to wear the yellow Star of David and thus be easily recognizable and often arrested.

Many Jews tried to go into hiding and many Aryans helped them, but it is impossible for a whole family to hide for ever when it is necessary to go out to get essential supplies.

One day I went with a colleague to pick up an old Jewish woman who had broken her pelvis. The Gestapo had just taken away her entire family, but she was considered too old to be bothered with. While the soldiers were searching the house the old grandmother was made, with the threat of a whip, to jump over small obstacles. This she could not do, so fell at the first and broke her pelvis. Neighbours who had witnessed the scene called the ambulance, but one can imagine the physical and mental anguish of this elderly lady.

All in all, life under German occupation was oppressive. Now, for the first time, we realized the value of freedom – freedom to publish, to travel, to buy food, to assemble for our own good purposes, to retain the products of our work, to trade freely. It was a German of an earlier and saner day, Schiller, who remarked that 'Freedom is the air of the spirit' – if only his successors had taken it to heart, but Schiller's ideas found little acceptance in the Third Reich. We now longed for an end to alien and hated uniforms in our streets and shops; an end to official

47

pronouncements, pasted on walls, in an alien and hated tongue; an end to the infinite number of limitations on our daily lives. The bulk of the nation was implacably determined not to give in, not to acquiesce meekly, to retain and assert our Belgian consciousness until the day when we should once again be free. It was to be four weary years before that long-awaited day. Like most of my fellow-citizens, I simply got on with my various jobs and kept my eyes constantly open for a chance to do anything which would strike a blow in the right cause.

As the days passed more people took their chance of putting their grain of sand in the well-oiled German machine – minor acts of sabotage increased: a lump of sugar in a petrol tank, a nail in a tyre, or even a cigarette burn in a German uniform when a packed tram created this opportunity.

Every time there was an anti-German incident, an act of sabotage, hostages were taken and many of these people were later shot; that, it was thought, would deter the dissidents from further such 'crimes'. Of course, it never did. One day the German police arrived at Jurbise and asked to see my father. Abruptly they commanded, 'You must come with us.'

He asked what it was about but received no answer, just a repetition of the order: 'You must come with us.'

My father was taken to the *Kommandantur* where he was told that, together with two other local notables, he was to travel daily in the train between Mons and Brussels in case of any possible 'incident'. If anything happened, they were told, all three would immediately be shot. So every morning, very early, my father would leave the house, saying cheerfully, 'See you tonight.' But my mother's heart would be heavy, knowing that for him that 'tonight' might never come. It was a week or two before the Germans abandoned the practice.

For spying, or helping Allied personnel, the penalty was to be shot or, worse still perhaps, be sent to a concentration camp. War is war. Many women were paying for their patriotism in German prisons or camps, and they were treated exactly as male prisoners. One of our agents, who was arrested, aged twenty-one, was expecting her first baby. Day after day she was interrogated and told that, if she did not give information about other agents, her husband would be shot in front of her. Several times she fainted and was revived by water thrown over her. At other times she was overcome by sickness, but she never gave in, and she told her torturers what she thought of them. No secrets passed her lips. In the end she was sent to Germany, where she miraculously survived. I

48

knew her only as Lysette, and it was through friends that I heard, after the war, of the happy ending: she and her child came home to a hero's welcome.

Every day seemed to bring us sad news. My father's sister, Comtesse Antoine d'Ursel, was sent to St Gilles prison when the departure of her husband for England was suspected. Sadly, as will be recalled later, he was working on an escape route and was drowned when helping people to cross the Bidassoa river into Spain.

Then there was the news, when we returned to Belgium in 1940, of the deaths of several of our dear friends who had been killed in the May campaign. I thought with sadness of the happy days when we used to dance together, and of the many parties at which we had all met. The loss of Manu de Formanoir and especially of Charles van der Burch saddened me greatly, as did that of Baudouin della Faille who died later in a concentration camp; many more deaths were to follow.*

Nevertheless, sabotage went on. Factories working for the Germans would find mysterious fires breaking out at irregular intervals. Arsonists hit at fuel dumps, railway marshalling yards, stockpiles of goods awaiting transportation to Germany. Trains, especially troop trains, would be derailed – seldom spectacularly, for in those early days explosives were not easily available – sufficiently often to cause widespread and long-lasting disruption of communications. Telephone cables laid by army signalling units would be cut and often the ends would be joined in such a way as to defy casual inspection, so that the interruption would only be located after much searching.

After any such act there would be thorough investigations – the word 'thorough', in this context, meaning that interrogation was often, in fact nearly always, accompanied by every device of fear and physical persuasion. Any culprits who could be identified would be executed, usually by firing squad. There were soon so many people under arrest that the Germans had to build a KZ** for them; this was at Breedonck. Here several deaths would be reported each day: people dying under torture, hostages executed by way of reprisal, those found guilty of sabotage. Older people told us that these excesses were just as bad as those committed in the earlier German war; yet the arson, the sabotage and the defiance went on, whatever the Germans might do by way of deterrence or revenge. Only liberation was to end it all.

By the end of 1940 there had been over a hundred major acts of

*see Appendix D.
**the usual abbreviation for concentration camp.

sabotage: German military installations and communications; petrol stores in the port of Antwerp; blast furnaces at Athus; factories in the Ardennes. Eight citizens of Liège had been executed for damaging electricity cables. Various salvage collections had been thwarted. Old newspapers were burned so that they could not be collected and recycled; the five-franc pieces, recalled for their nickel content, were simply buried to await better times.

The canals were favourite targets: lock gates were easily damaged and later, when dynamite was more available, considerable damage was possible to sluice gates and dams. At one such site a carload of Gestapo agents arrived to investigate, but when they later returned to their car, they found that it was unserviceable: all four tyres had been slashed.

And the incidents continued, as did the savage reprisals. Small wonder that a historian, writing in later years, said: 'Of all the countries which resisted Nazi tyranny, Belgium probably faced the greatest difficulties, achieved the greatest success and paid the highest price.'* That highest price, however grievous, did not succeed in preventing anti-German incidents of every kind.

In an air battle over Wavre, six RAF men were killed. In spite of German orders to the contrary, an immense crowd attended the funeral; there were masses of flowers, and a cross on the grave carried the inscription, 'In gratitude to those who have given their lives for our deliverance'. Another aircraft was shot down near Gembloux; the crew was killed. Again, great crowds attended the funeral and all shops in the town closed for the morning. The Germans, infuriated, fired blanks over the heads of the crowd, who dispersed only slowly. Such graves were lovingly and regularly tended, and always carried fresh flowers; such acts of gratitude, however, had to be carried out at night, but despite the danger there was no lack of volunteers.

No German, at any level, could have had the slightest doubt about the attitude of the Belgians to their temporary masters. Having failed to win co-operation by correctness, the Germans tried increasing doses of fear: every day people were arrested on the faintest kind of suspicion. Occasionally General von Falkenhausen was asked to help: he was a man of breeding and culture and we credited him with a sense of justice – even, sometimes, a certain kindness. But he was heard to say to a Belgian, 'You should know by now that any Gestapo corporal can order me around,' a statement which was soon general knowledge.

On one occasion when the Gestapo headquarters in Brussels was

Secret Forces of World War II, P. Warner

50

strafed by Jean de Selys, flying from England, the local people came out on the street and demonstrated their delight; the Gestapo were furious. General Dieudonné, a celebrated Belgian veteran of World War I, was caught laughing his head off and the Gestapo forced him to clean public lavatories for a week. A young daughter of the Mérode family was savagely beaten with the buckle of a German belt and an elderly priest was forced to bend over a table and was beaten into unconsciousness. A woman was dragged by the hair through the streets and then forced to strip naked in public. Von Falkenhausen was 'not available' and his second-in-command told the Red Cross, 'There is nothing we can do.'

To understand the bewildering situation in Belgium in 1940–41 one has to look at three phases.

First: the capitulation and the period to the summer of 1940, when most people were totally confused; the war had not followed the pattern of World War I and there was a total political void. Strangely enough, the Communist Party was allowed to function, although closely watched, until 22 June 1941 when the Russo-German pact was broken and the Germans started their Russian campaign. The three traditional (national) political parties, the Centrist Catholics, the right-wing Liberals and the left-wing Socialists, which together represented 75 per cent of the Parliament, were not allowed any activity. Leon Degrelle, the leader of the Rexistes, was permitted to hold meetings in Brussels and in the French-speaking part of the country, but he had very little following in the Flemish part of the country because he was a French-language speaker. The Germans encouraged two political trends to develop in Flanders: the Flemish Nationalist Party (VNV), and a small group of fanatics who were wholehearted Nazi supporters (the LLAC movement). Hitler, as documentation later proved, wanted, after victory, to absorb the Flemish part of Belgium as part of the 'Greater Reich' concept, thus controlling the Channel ports. He also wanted to reclaim the provinces of Eupen and Malmedy, taken from Germany in 1918.

Second: the period between the summer of 1940 and the spring of 1941 when there was a limited movement towards collaboration, but the shortage of food, and especially the elation caused by the Battle of Britain, and the evident determination of the English people, rekindled hope in the occupied countries.

Third: the period which started on 22 June 1941, after the Germans had invaded Russia. The Belgians felt that, even if the Germans had some initial success, they would eventually come to grief, as Napoleon had. Thousands of Belgians remained prisoners of war. The British were holding firm. It was during this phase of the war that the announcement that in 'captivity' the King had quietly remarried, brought shock and great disappointment to his supporters, and bitterness among families who had lonely relatives in prisoner-of-war camps.* Because of this the Belgian government in London gained more credibility and attention.

I would like to say that there was no collaboration during these times but, sadly, there was some. Some industrialists kept their factories going, to employ men who would otherwise have been sent to Germany, but a few others saw it was good business for them to keep in with the Germans. The Comte de Launoy was thought by many to be one of these. There was Henri de Man, considered to be too near to the King, who fancied for himself a role in government. Then there were the traitors who made money by collaboration and, as in all wars, the women who either sold themselves to the Boche or fell in love with the handsome German soldiers. They were to pay dearly for their mistake or treachery.

Of course, most people just went on living as best they could and, from 1940 to the liberation in 1944, there were many stories of resistance and of suffering. These can be multiplied indefinitely and verified by unimpeachable witnesses.

As the course of the war turned against the Germans, after I had left Belgium, the occupying power got tougher and harder with the Belgian population. My parents were thrown out of their home. My mother went to the local convent and my father, after he was released from being a hostage, stayed with a nearby farmer. Of my brothers, John was still a prisoner of war, Xavier was forced to work in a coal-mine, Alain was allowed to organize food production on the estate at Jurbise, Francis finished his studies in Brussels, and my youngest brother, Philippe, was away at school. My sister Bee continued with her work in the Motor Corps. In 1941, however, all these events were still to come; each of us was getting on with the job of living from day to day.

*His bride was Lilian Baels, aged twenty-five (to his forty-one).

4

The Underground

FROM the very start of the German occupation, as I have indicated, attempts at resistance sprang up. Initially, inevitably, such defiance consisted of spontaneous and unco-ordinated actions, carried out by ordinary citizens everywhere as opportunity offered, but by the end of 1940 some kind of organization was slowly coming into being.

I found myself, due to the circumstances of my family playing host to the Italian Air Force, involved with intelligence gathering, specializing in aviation matters. True, I worked for two full days a week for the Motor Corps and quite frequently at a canteen for debilitated children (Cantine Leopold III), in a suburb of Brussels, but all this activity still left me with ample time to carry out specific tasks for my section of the underground.

I was assigned to work as number two to my friend, Baron Albert Kervyn de Lettenhove, who was known as K1. Names were hidden behind such cryptic designations so that as few of us as possible knew the identities of our contacts: if we were picked up and interrogated we could not then betray our friends.* To the Gestapo, 'interrogation' had wide possibilities. It was quite common for suspects to have fingers and toes dislocated, or their finger- and toe-nails would be pulled out. Should these measures not produce the desired effect, teeth would be drilled down to the jaw bone. A minor torture was to feed a suspect salted food and then refuse any form of drink, or to make him – or her – stand for hours on end, facing a wall, with occasional heavy blows to the back of the head, so that the face was driven heavily against the wall; this resulted in broken noses and teeth, and split lips. It took impossible determination to endure all this and still not talk, yet there were brave

*see Appendix E.

men and women who managed to do just that. If, then, the torturers decided that they had nothing to lose by the death of a suspect, the final sanction was delayed strangulation by intermittent hanging.

The first admitted execution was on 12 August 1941, though since long before then people had been 'disappearing', never to be seen again. Between that date and the end of January 1942 there were another fifty-six *notified* executions for various offences: assisting British airmen, possession of leaflets or of weapons, sabotage; and there continued to be many people who just vanished into German gaols and were never seen again.

We could not have known initially, of course, to what lengths the enemy would go to crack down on resistance, but as the months went by some details leaked out – a few fortunate souls actually returned to tell the horrifying tale – and this served only to stiffen our anger and our purpose.

K1 was the head of the aviation section, which I later took over from him. Our group was called 'Service Zero'. Albert was, and has remained, an extremely shrewd man with great qualities of character; his dash, bravery and resolve were to be severely tested and proved in the months ahead. At the time of my own recruitment he had already organized a network of agents covering most of the major airfields and I was slotted into those. He had also achieved the equally difficult job of establishing lines of communication so that intelligence could be passed along for final transmission to England. New agents were constantly being selected, recruited and trained.

At first we made many mistakes. We knew too many of our field workers by their real names and indeed we were too trustful. I remember with sadness one of our men. He was a gendarme, and so was well placed to collect information. In time he came under suspicion; soon he was tortured and he cracked, implicating others of his group who were subsequently arrested by the Germans. Fortunately, each individual group worked in isolation from other such groups, so the damage, bad as it was, was limited.

Sometimes the Germans managed to infiltrate a 'plant': a Belgian who had decided to serve the enemy. He would carry out his duties for a time, while he amassed as much information as possible about the organization in which he was working. Then one morning there would be a series of co-ordinated raids: men and women would be taken from their homes to an unknown and menacing future. When this happened we felt for our friends, knowing what they would be undergoing and of

54

the grief of their families. It was not possible to predict what kind of person could resist torture: sometimes a huge, burly man would crack, whereas a smaller man or woman, although suffering appalling treatment, would refuse to reveal anything. As I have said, throughout 1940 and early 1941 we knew very few of the details of standard Gestapo treatment, but we learned to extend our network, to use only ciphers, to avoid direct contact with other agents as far as possible and to make use of a range of passwords. So each group was small and each member knew at most only his own immediate contact, and even then only by a code-name. In this manner we hoped to limit the damage caused by the arrest of any individual agent.

By 1941 the plan of our organization was as follows:

Courtrai Region
Airfields at Wewelghem   Controlled by B1 in Mouscron,
            Moorseel   together with L3, who worked at the
            Bondues   French/Belgian frontier, and X, who
                           was an airfield worker at
                           Wewelghem

St Trond Region
Airfields at Brusthem   Controlled by L. Lambrechts,
            Tirlemont   together with three sub-agents
            St Trond

Brussels Region
Airfields at Evère   Controlled by I18 together with
            Melsbroeck   several sub-agents

Beauvechain Region
Airfields at Les Burettes   Controlled by L, in Jodoigne,
            Jauche   together with three sub-agents

Chièvres Region
Airfield at   Chièvres   Controlled by T1, together with two
                         sub-agents – *agents volants* – who
                         did not live in the area

There were also airfields at St Denis Westeren, controlled by H7, from Ghent; at St Nicholas Waes, controlled by an agent who worked in a local shop; at Aeltre, controlled by IF; and at Deurne (near Antwerp), controlled by an army officer.

In March 1941 I met Claude de Villermont, who was a relative of mine. Claude was then working near his home in Boussu, collecting weapons left behind by the French army and hiding them in the woods of the Ardennes, for use by the Resistance. He was then just sixteen years old, not very tall, with a frank and open face and an ever-ready smile, and in his last year at college, at Maredsous. He had had diphtheria and while recuperating was supposed to be working at home. He was the despair of his parents, failing more often than not to turn up for classes with his tutor. His parents could not be allowed, for reasons of their own safety, to know about his membership of the Resistance, in which he was very active. Activity, they thought, was foreign to his nature and they reproached him bitterly and often for shirking his lessons. To all this, of course, he was not able to reply. As a small boy he had been delicate and nervous, but now he had developed into a young man of exceptional bravery; danger attracted him and he seemed to be completely fearless. In our group he was awarded the code-name 'Valiant'. I asked Claude if he would work for me, gathering intelligence about the airfields and troop movements in the region near his home. It was an area which he knew very well. He agreed to do this, and carried out his intelligence gathering with tremendous energy and courage; later he became the personal courier of the head of our organization, Charles Woeste. At a later date still, Claude and I both escaped to Britain and, during the Normandy campaign, he was parachuted into Belgium to help co-ordinate the local military forces behind the lines. Later he rejoined the Belgian army, and sadly was killed in the last days of the final push in the Ardennes: Claude's jeep took a direct hit from a mortar bomb and he was killed instantly. He was only twenty then; Belgium could ill afford to lose such a young man.

During most of 1941 my work for the aviation section of Service Zero took me through most of Belgium and sometimes into northern France. I usually travelled by bicycle, and sometimes the journey would be long enough to keep me away from home for a night or even two nights. My job was to keep watch on airfields. The Germans often changed the main airfields they used, in an attempt to foil British bombing raids or even sabotage attacks. Sometimes they extended an existing airfield, bringing in more and different types of aircraft; sometimes they closed down operational airfields, or even laid out dummy airfields to attract attacks. A mock village would be built, with all kinds of buildings – even a 'church' – all in cardboard and plywood. Trees would be simulated and a dummy runway would be marked out. All such activity had to be carefully monitored and reported.

One of my first jobs took me to Mouscron, to find out what was happening in that region and, especially, at the airfield near there. Large-scale construction works had apparently begun and we were always very alert for such activity. Following the instructions given me by K1, I went to No. 5 in the main square, the Grande Place; this was a hardware store. I went in and asked to see Madame as I had an order I wished to place.

A woman of about forty-five or so appeared; she seemed to be intelligent and bright, and looked at me enquiringly. I gave the agreed password: 'Can you supply me with some vegetables?' (not likely to have been hit on accidentally by any innocent customer in a hardware shop). She immediately beckoned me into a back room; for a few minutes we made general conversation while she summed me up, and then we got down to the work. This lady, code-name B1, had a particularly important job in her part of the country, controlling sub-agents in Wewelghem, Moorseel and other places. She was also charged with watching train movements between Belgium and France, as Mouscron was on the frontier. Troop trains were obviously of special interest to us, as were trains of open flat-tops, carrying military vehicles of all kinds, guns – especially flak* – and searchlights. Her real name, I knew, was Madame de Berdt; she had an uncle who in World War I had worked with the famous Louise de Bettignies, and Madame de Berdt had heard many stories of the work and adventures of that intrepid woman. Clearly, she had also absorbed much useful advice. B1 was already known to be brave and indefatigable, but also prudent and calm always.

She knew her region very well, of course, so we decided to go together the next day to see exactly what was happening at Moorseel. I spent that night at the local hotel, using an assumed name backed by an illicit identity card which had been issued to me, and the next morning we set off on bicycles. The weather was terrible that day; the airfield was only ten miles away but by the time we reached it we were both soaked through and plastered with mud thrown up by passing vehicles or even our own wheels. We cycled slowly past the airfield, memorizing carefully everything we could see and identifying the types of German aircraft parked on the tarmac or around the perimeter of the field. Later we put our heads together and prepared a careful and comprehensive list.

This part of our job finished, we left for Reckem to meet L3, one of the sub-agents. He lived in a small workman's house, rather isolated but

*An acronym for the German words for anti-aircraft guns.

57

on higher ground, so that he was well able with binoculars to watch the comings and goings at the Wewelghem airfield, which was his designated target. He was not our only helper there; we had also an agent, known to us as 'Red Head', who was employed locally by the Germans. L3 was very much involved in frequent crossings of the frontier; he would take out or bring back messages and intelligence summaries or, on occasion, even explosives needed for a specific operation. He had all sorts of ways of getting across, knowing the area as he did. One Sunday, for instance, he crossed the frontier accompanied by his wife and pushing their baby in a pram: the family were supposedly off to see an aunt living in Roubaix. They were so obviously a harmless family group that they hardly merited more than the merest glance from the customs officials; one quick look at their identity cards and they were through. Those same frontier officials would have been most surprised if they had accompanied the family into a café a mile past the frontier; in a back room, secure from prying eyes, the baby was taken out of the pram and a box of TNT was removed from under the baby's seat. The resourceful and brave L3, whose real name was Leleu, went on working for us until his sight began to fail – a consequence of prolonged malnutrition. Then his wonderful wife simply stepped in and took over his job. They knew well the risks involved and what the Germans would do to them if either of them was caught in any underground activity, yet still they persisted. Their courage and patriotism excite boundless admiration.

On this particular day at Moorseel we were able to report that the runway had been extended and some extra building work was in progress: airfield facilities of some kind. The numbers of He 111s and Do 215s had increased, and a fighter unit seemed to be in the process of moving in; all very useful information. This would be taken back to Brussels and handed over to K1 as quickly as I could get it to him; such intelligence, together with news of petrol and ammunition dumps, and the location of German units, would be sent to England by radio. Our main transmitter was in Boitsfort and was operated by Comte Jean d'Ursel and his wife. These transmissions had to be as short as possible to prevent the Germans taking cross bearings.

To pass information from agent to agent along the line of communication we used a system of letter boxes. For example, the agent at Mouscron, B1, would send someone to Brussels with the information written on very fine paper and hidden in the bottom of a packet of cigarettes or perhaps of a matchbox. On a prearranged day, Albert Kervyn or I would go to a little café in Brussels, the Faux Pas, and ask for a drink.

58

That would give me the chance to inspect the other customers, to see whether there might be a suspicious character there; in this we were aided by the fact that Gestapo thugs usually wore trilby-type hats, long grey or dark green overcoats and, often, high boots. It seems never to have occurred to them that their restricted choice of civilian clothing itself constituted a recognizable uniform.

Belgian traitors – mercifully there were very few of them – were almost impossible to detect. Any single man, obviously taking his time for no particular reason, was suspect. I did nothing in a hurry but if my careful inspection was reassuring, I would ask whether a parcel had arrived for Madame Marie Tirlemont – my identity for the day. In proof of this I had a genuine identity card, with authentic signature and stamp, but testifying to my new identity. The young woman at the counter would say 'Sorry. Nothing for you', and at the same time hand me a box of matches to light my cigarette. In this box would be a scrap of paper on which would be the information I had come to collect; within a few minutes I would leave for home, where I would read the message before passing it on or acting on it, whichever seemed necessary. Another letter box was a milliner who had her shop in a quiet street of Brussels. When I recruited her I thought that her business would explain the comings and goings to her house and that she would be reasonably safe. Her name was Madame Snauwaert, a widower with a young daughter.

One of the main agents in our group was Jacques Pinte, whom I already knew slightly from earlier and happier days. He became, and remained until his untimely death in January 1987, a very good friend. He had a marvellous sense of humour; he never flapped, even when things were tough and apparent disaster was looming; he was extremely brave, as his many decorations testified. He was the best kind of *camarade* to have in a difficult world. He had a delightful wife whom he adored; she accepted his comings and goings and even his occasional absences for days on end if the needs of the service demanded it. On one occasion Jacques and I made a special expedition to the airfield at Deurne; the local agent had reported a great deal of work being done at night, all activity ceasing during daylight hours. Runways were being extended, petrol dumps were being moved and a new type of aircraft had been seen taking off and landing. All this called for a detailed inspection; we left Brussels one day by train and that same evening reached the vicinity of the airfield. Without being observed, we thought, we hid in the high grass and bushes around the barbed-wire perimeter fence;

59

from here we could see the work which was going on by the light of floodlights. We were able to identify the Do 215s on the tarmac, together with a new single-engined fighter – later to be identified as the FW 190.

Suddenly, Jacques pressed my arm; he had heard the sound of an approaching German patrol. He murmured, 'Lie down quickly. Pretend we're lovers.' We must have put on a convincing act, in spite of our anxiety, because when the patrol stopped nearby we heard only lewd laughter and fairly obvious comments from the soldiers. They were searching for spies but had found only two young people lying in the grass. We were told to leave immediately, but by then we had all the information we had come so far to collect. Fortunately we managed to get back to Brussels without any further alarms and our observations were passed on in the usual way.

On another occasion we found ourselves late one evening in a remote area and had to spend the night at a local farm. There was only one spare bedroom and in it only the one bed. It was agreed that I would have the bed while Jacques would sleep – if sleep were possible – on the sofa; this item looked far from comfortable. In the middle of the night I awoke and looked over: the poor man was shivering with the cold. After all, it was a large bed. I said, 'I'm not offering to share my bed with you but you can come over and sleep under the eiderdown.'

'You mean,' he answered, 'that tonight I must become a kind of monk?'

'That's exactly what I do mean.'

'All right then.'

And he was.

Occasionally, when two people were needed to do a special job, I was joined by Guillaume, Comte de Limburg-Stirum, although he was not officially a member of our section.

As I have said, most of my duties had to do with airfields, yet I was often sent on other missions for the group. On one occasion I had to go to my grandparents' château at Vlamertinghe, near Ypres, the scene of so much hard fighting in the First World War. As a child, together with my brothers and sister, I had spent a month of every summer here with my du Parc grandparents, and I knew every nook and cranny of this large building. It was a particularly exciting place for children as there were several hidden staircases and passages; behind the door of the pantry there was a sliding panel which led to a flight of stairs. At the top was a small room, seldom used but steeped in mystery. Under the carpet of my grandfather's study was a trapdoor which gave on to another unused room: what purpose it might ever have served I do not know – but what a house it was for children playing hide-and-seek!

The large attics were a favourite roosting place for owls, which found their way in somehow although attempts were made to close off any means of ingress. Their movements during the hours of darkness suggested mysterious beings creeping around, and their mournful hoots were always frightening – deliciously so – to young children. In each of the towers was what seemed to be an endless spiral stair and when one eventually reached the top one could imagine oneself suspended in space, high above the countryside.

The château is now lived in by my cousins, Maurice and Titane du Parc, who have made it into a museum of Victorian furniture and effects; it is a happy place where all the family like to gather.* In those days of war, however, it had been requisitioned as a headquarters by the Germans; but they did allow our family to retain the rooms in one of the wings, even though the château stood dangerously close to the forbidden coastal zone. From Dunkirk to the little resort of Le Zoute, near the Dutch frontier, the Germans had constructed a strong line of defences. The coast is a long succession of sandy beaches backed by sanddunes; at low tide those beaches offered a level, firm surface almost half a mile deep and ideal for a landing from the sea. The beaches themselves were covered with obstacles designed to stop landing-craft, tanks and other vehicles. The cottages of the beach resorts, which run in an unbroken line for almost fifty miles, were gutted and turned into well-camouflaged pill-boxes and gun emplacements. Mines were laid in the dunes and on the beaches. One stormy night, hardly the weather for an invasion, the waves were rolling high up the beach and pounding down with great force; as a result mines were detonating all along the coast. There was a great panic; the garrison turned out and armoured units began to move into position until one German, brighter than the others, correctly diagnosed the cause of all the *brouhaha*. Yet, before calm had been restored several of the defenders had been killed, either by their own mines or by trigger-happy comrades.

A few miles back from the coast there was a second line of defence, less well camouflaged. There was even talk of a proposed third line, further back still, but of this last we knew very little.

The whole area was closed to all civilians except those who lived there and a few bringing supplies to the local shops. Of course, we were well

*Sadly, Maurice died suddenly in May 1981.

informed about what was going on and the important details were passed on to London. We did not always understand the full significance of what we were reporting: the launching sites for the V1 and V2 were a mystery to us, but we passed on the information nevertheless.

On the night of 19 August 1942 I was at Vlamertinghe, together with my brothers Alain and Francis. We had gone this time primarily to replenish our food supplies: food was easier to obtain in Flanders than in Brussels; incidentally, I would be able to carry out one of the regular checks on the German troops in residence (the units changed from time to time). I would also be able to monitor troop movements in the surrounding areas; the military markings on the vehicles using local roads were a good indication of units stationed nearby, and close monitoring enabled us to build up a picture of comings and goings. In the early hours of the morning I left my room and silently made my way along the familiar corridors to one of the drawing-rooms, which the Germans had converted into an office. With a well-shaded torch I was inspecting some of the papers when suddenly I heard someone snoring and realized that there was a soldier asleep in the small ante-room which led out of it. I froze with horror, then crept quietly out and began to make my way back to my room. I was nearly back there when there was an almighty commotion and the whole château was suddenly full of light, noise and movement. I dashed the remainder of the way, fortunately without being seen, and waited, trembling. What on earth could be happening?

Outside, car engines were racing; men were shouting; there were running footsteps both outside and inside the building. The question was: why? An hour or so later we found out. The Allies had made a raid on Dieppe, only some one hundred and fifty miles to the west of us, and there was intense fighting in progress, on land, on sea and in the air. The purpose was, of course, to test the German defences and to exercise landing tactics; as a lesson the undertaking was expensive in terms of lives – mainly Canadian lives. The Germans, of course, acclaimed it as a great victory, but there can be no doubt that the bloody lessons learned that day were of value when the long-awaited Normandy invasion came about, almost two years later.

However, there we were in the château, surrounded by shouting Germans running this way and that in great agitation. There is no doubt that they thought the invasion proper had commenced and, a hundred and fifty miles away or not, they were taking every precaution. Men were running in long files, like agitated ants defending their hill, carrying waste-paper baskets; the contents would be tipped on a bonfire in the garden and the bearers would scurry back for more files, more documents, more code books. Their haste was such that many of the papers drifted downwind in the heat of the flames, no more than scorched at the edges, and came to rest in the nearest shrubbery. Later that morning my brothers and I armed ourselves with sharpened sticks and made an expedition, ostensibly to find and destroy the nests of the local wasps, which had in fact been particularly troublesome that year. We hovered near the smoking ashes of the fire and picked up as many papers as still seemed legible. I reasoned that if the Germans thought them important enough to destroy, then their contents must be of interest to the Allies.

Slowly, calm reasserted itself. When news came through, a few hours later, that the Allied troops were withdrawing, there was manifest relief: toasts were drunk, heels were clicked and hands were raised in salute. Just wait, we thought: just you wait. When the real thing happens it won't be over as quickly and as easily as that. We held on to that thought during the next few days, while the German press and radio gave out their endless shouts of triumph; *we* had seen the master-race with its guard down.

From the beginning of 1942 onwards we had been getting requests from England for information about coastal defences and, especially, about unusual constructions being built just behind the Belgian and Dutch coastlines. At the time we did not understand what we were reporting, though there was no doubt of the importance attached to our reports. These constructions were, of course, the launching sites for the V1 pilotless aircraft and the V2 rockets, both still at the planning stage. The area immediately behind the coast was, as I have said, forbidden to all civilians except those actually living there, but the underground groups had many contacts among these people.

In 1942 I was given a detailed map of the coastal defences and of the construction sites, and was ordered to take it to Paris. My cover story for the journey was that I was going to call on relations there, though in fact I had resolved not to visit them: some of them were pro-Pétain and therefore inclined to be anti-British. How anti-British I could not tell, but certainly I dared take no chances. Yet it was not surprising that some of the French were taken in by talk of the 'New Order'. In 1937 and 1938 there had been quite dreadful riots in Paris and there had been some danger of the Communists launching a *coup d'état*. Great anxiety was caused to many people, especially the more prosperous and the bourgeoisie. Now Pétain was the head of the French government and most people trusted completely that a *maréchal* of France could only have the real interests of the French people at heart. They forgot that Pétain was a very old, very vain man, who did not always understand clearly what was happening or that he was being manipulated by others – especially by his prime minister, Pierre Laval. Many Frenchmen were shocked and angered by the British attempts to take over and immobilize the French fleet. The fleet was widely distributed: some units were already in British harbours, others were in Alexandria, the Antilles, Casablanca, Dakar and Algiers. But the most important part of the fleet was at Mers el Kebir, among them, no fewer than four battleships. Britain was concerned that none of these ships should come into German possession: Laval was not to be trusted – he was capable, the British thought, of striking a deal with the Germans. If the enemy possessed themselves of these major units, the whole balance of sea power would change.

In the first few days of July 1941 Britain took action. In most of the bases the French ships were disarmed; in Dakar the *Richelieu* was disabled by gunfire; but in Mers el Kebir there was a full-scale battle. Most of the French ships there were destroyed or disabled; thirteen hundred French seamen died and many more were wounded. The French, who had promised that none of their ships would ever be handed over to the Germans, saw this as an act of treachery by an ally and were bitter. Some echoes of that bitterness have survived even to the present day. As a retaliation, and as a sign of their fury, French aircraft carried out a bombing raid on Gibraltar, after which efforts were made on both sides not to exacerbate the situation.

The German propaganda machine had a field day and many more of the French were understandably ready to listen. Yet in time the voice of the Free French, broadcast daily from England, was instrumental in winning over the hearts and minds of many, or even most, French people. De Gaulle grew steadily more popular and feelings against the Vichy government grew stronger.

There were many jokes circulating about Pétain and Darlan, the strongly anti-British navy minister in Pétain's cabinet. In one shop I saw a poster with photographs of the two men. Under that of Pétain was the laconic verdict *'épuisé'* (washed out) and under the other *'vendu'* (sold out).

Above all, the voice of Churchill (despite his execrable French accent) was an inspiration to the people of occupied Europe. He was the

64

inspiration which brought more and more French men and women to assist the work of the various Resistance groups.

So I could understand why my French relatives felt as they did; our meeting, I decided, would have to wait for happier days.

The map which was given to me was too large to be concealed in my usual hiding place: a silver cross, of which the bottom unscrewed; so I tucked the map carefully away in my underwear. There would be the usual German check-point *en route,* always nerve-racking, and my papers would hardly escape for long if I were to be body-searched by one of the gimlet-eyed, massively built females who worked for German security. However, needs must. I caught an early morning train from Brussels. The round trip would take a day; four hours or so each way, with a few hours to meet my contacts. Passwords were exchanged and the papers handed over and we parted. Neither of us knew the identity of the other and it was best so. Then I spent a few hours wandering about well-known streets, looking into shop windows now empty and trying to overlook the numerous German uniforms and the sound of German voices.

The train journey to Paris with documents on me was an anxious one; as the German control worked its way down the train the door of the compartment slid open and in came a uniformed German and a civilian. The latter did not speak; he looked carefully at each passenger, a look which I, at least, interpreted as menacing. I felt I was being closely assessed. Then they were gone and the door slid shut again. There was more than one sigh of relief as the train rolled on.

Luckily the journey home was totally uneventful and I was in my bed in the early hours of the following morning, before anyone stirred. Nobody even knew that I had been away and so no questions were asked. It was better that the family should not know about my underground work; my work in the Motor Corps and in the children's canteen was an adequate explanation for my activities.

As I have said earlier, most of our information was sent to London by radio; occasionally, as above, documents could be got out via France, but usually messages would be coded and transmitted. Of course we had to transmit from different locations to avoid being fixed by German direction-finding equipment and this taxed our ingenuity. One group had recruited a mobile radio repairer who would transmit from scattered locations while on his rounds; the transmitter was hidden behind a secret panel in his van. To check and analyse our information, almost every week I would meet the head of Service Zero, Charles Woeste. He was a lawyer with a practice in Brussels, very intelligent, indefatigable in his information-gathering activities and obviously very brave. Sadly he came under suspicion; one day he was arrested and sent to a concentration camp; but he survived and came back to us at the end of the war. Together we used to study the different reports and extract the vital details; sometimes we had to ask agents for more specific information as they did not always understand the importance of the news that they were supplying. But we had no doubt that everything which we could report would be fitted in to the bigger picture 'over there'; the occasional coded messages in return, appreciating our efforts, were enough to keep us going.*

Sometimes my work took me to Antwerp and here I would stay with my great friends Geneviève and Charles Bracht.** Charles had a small boat, fitted with an outboard motor, and we would take it out on the River Schelde ostensibly on a pleasure trip when in fact we were on the alert to note, interpret and memorize any enemy movements on or near the river. One day Geneviève and I got into a garage where military vehicles were kept and while I kept watch, she went from lorry to lorry, inspecting the log books. My heart was in my mouth as she worked her way around, but we were not interrupted and managed to leave without having been noticed at all. We missed no single chance to add to our store of information: wherever we went and whatever we were doing, our eyes were always open. When the RAF, and later the USAAF, were engaged in the massive bombing campaign against Germany, we were asked to locate and keep up-dated the location of all flak and searchlight positions. Such things were hard to hide and a constant stream of information went back to London.

At night, increasingly, the sirens would wail; what few lights there were – in marshalling yards, for example – would be switched off; into the silence would obtrude the distant, then growing, noise of aircraft engines. That welcome sound never failed to thrill us: it was the herald of eventual freedom. We learned to distinguish the noise of a Wellington from that of a Mosquito; later we heard the four-engined Halifaxes and Lancasters come over. There would be gunfire, sometimes far away and then somewhere closer at hand; the searchlights would stab the night

---

*see Appendix C.
**Charles was kidnapped, presumably for ransom, in 1981, and was shot dead when he tackled his kidnapper. After weeks of agonizing uncertainty for his wife and children, his body was found. Later the criminal was caught, tried and imprisoned.

sky; inevitably, some of our friends up there would be hit and we knew that our countrymen working on the escape routes would be busy. The planes droned over in their hundreds, night after night, and in the morning we would watch the faces of the young German soldiers and of their officers. Their reaction was in itself a possible news item for us. Sometimes they were very silent, a tense silence broken by outbursts of irritation, tirades of abuse, swearing at the slightest incident. The Italians had long gone from Jurbise, to their obvious relief, and we now had Germans billeted on us. I remember one young officer who spoke very little; he lived in a different world, a defeated world, packed with sorrow. He came from Duisburg and we knew that the city was a regular target for Allied bombers.

In order to minimize the risks of being caught, and of mutual implication should we be caught, the different underground organizations – military intelligence, sabotage, escape lines – worked generally quite separately. Only under orders or in an emergency did we co-operate. On two occasions I was asked to look after British airmen. One had been shot down near Namur and had to be moved quickly as several planes had been brought down and the Germans were certain to carry out large-scale searches of the district. The airman knew not a single word of French so he had to be thoroughly briefed in English before he could be moved from the farm where he was concealed. Then I had to escort him across a bridge over the River Meuse; such bridges were always guarded, but he had to be got over to a safe house ten miles further on.

He had been given civilian clothes and had been instructed how not to draw attention to himself by a false move or word. We set off arm in arm, pretending to keep up a conversation in French. He nodded and smiled at intervals, though he did not understand a single word. I knew that there was always the danger that a young man like himself could be snatched up by a German press-gang and taken off to captivity in Germany. But we must have put on a convincing act for I was able to hand him over at his safe house to the Comet Line, one of the most successful of all the escape organizations. He was very grateful; I had been glad of the chance to talk English again and was thrilled to hear up-to-the-minute news of daily life in England: how people lived, what they thought and felt, what things were scarce.

On another occasion I was told that a British airman was being hidden on a farm near Marienburg. His plane had been hit and had caught fire but he had parachuted to safety; unfortunately, he had been so badly

67

burned that he could not see where he was landing. The farmer, Mr Flandre, and his family took him in and called a local doctor, whom they knew they could trust. For several weeks the airman stayed on the farm, having his burns attended to until he would be fit enough to begin his long journey home. The farmer, of course, knew that he would be shot if an Allied airman was caught there.

Three of us decided to take the airman on to Dinant: Villermont, whose home was nearby, Jacques Pinte and myself. At Dinant we would contact an evacuation line. We got to the farm one evening to a huge welcome by the Flandre family, and from the airman, who was overjoyed at the thought of returning to England. His burns were still visible but they had healed well. He had spent many hours in his hideout, carving beautiful model aircraft out of wood; they seemed to indicate his strong wish to get home and resume flying.

Early the following morning the four of us boarded the train for Dinant. Because of the shortage of rolling-stock, trains were always overcrowded and we found ourselves in a packed compartment. The other travellers were obviously local people going to work or shopping. We had warned our airman, who was in civilian clothes and using a scarf to hide his burns as much as possible, that he must not utter a single word. But he was young, and happy to be on his way home, and he either did not understand or totally forgot the necessity for silence. Suddenly he burst out talking in English. We were alarmed, but the other occupants of the compartment were good people who just smiled: it was totally obvious to them who our young man was.

At Dinant we took him to a villa where a prearranged signal, an upturned table in the garden, told us that the coast was clear. We went in with him to say goodbye and to wish him good luck.

The owner of the villa said, 'You are lucky. You have come at just the right time. They have left.'

'What do you mean?'

'The Gestapo were here yesterday morning. There was nobody here except myself and they could find nothing suspicious, so they left,' he told us.

Later, we heard, our airman reached home safely.

Those years in occupied Belgium were very busy for me, but they were also exciting years. As time went by the radio told us of the American entry into the war, of the battles in North Africa and of the fighting on the Eastern Front, and we realized anew each day how important it was that we just keep going: we, too, were part of this immense machine in however humble a way. The tide had turned in favour of the Allies and our spirits were high – but the difficulties had not diminished.

So much for our Resistance work; what of daily life in our occupied Belgium?

Gradually, people came to see clearly that despite the German successes of 1940 and 1941, from North Cape to the Pyrenees, from Biscay to Crete, they would eventually come to grief, even as Napoleon had done. More and more Belgians joined the various arms of the Resistance movement, encouraged by Britain's indomitable stand (expressed unmistakably as I have said, in Churchill's speeches) and by growing hatred of the German brutality and oppression. We were also enraged, perhaps unfairly or illogically, by the fact that so many Belgians remained prisoners of war.

The sad plight of the Jewish people was becoming ever more noticeable. From 1941 they were compelled to wear the yellow Star of David and often some would be rounded up, to disappear without trace. Various details of the concentration camps were leaking through, but we never knew how many of these to believe: surely no twentieth-century European nation would or could carry through so dreadful a pogrom?

Yet one day I was waiting with Loulou de Wouters at the Gare du Nord in Brussels. We had an ambulance and were there to pick up some patients who were due to arrive by train. That day, I remember, we had parked by one of the little-used sidings. A train came in and stopped a little distance away, where it would be rather isolated from all the usual bustle of the station. There seemed nothing very special about this train, just the usual string of cattle-trucks, and we barely noticed its arrival.

Suddenly Loulou said to me, 'Can you hear what I hear?'

I strained my ears and was conscious of a low moaning sound, eerie and disquieting. 'There's a strange noise,' I replied, 'like someone in distress.'

Very carefully we moved nearer to the train, from which the noise seemed to emanate; gradually it became obvious to both of us that the noise we could hear was the sound of many people, moaning. Now we could hear another noise, perhaps many children, weeping.

It dawned on us that these trucks were full of people, mainly Jewish we supposed, on their way to Germany. We had heard that they were often transported in this way, but only now did we realize the full horror of it all; there before our eyes were these moving mass coffins.

We felt sick and full of pity for our fellow-humans, so appallingly treated, and frustrated, too, that there was no way in which we could help these wretched people. We looked at each other and one of us (it could equally well have been either) said, 'This is unforgivable. We will never forget this.'

Then we saw the first German faces turning our way – a few Germans in uniform were standing in small groups here and there on the platform – and we thought it prudent to wander casually away. But the memory of that day will always be with me.

In October 1942 the Germans decreed that all men and women between eighteen and thirty-five years of age were liable to be sent to work in Germany (by 1943 women were exempted from this law). The local councils were ordered to draw up lists of all those thus liable and not doing essential work. Of course, the staffs did their best to falsify or to hide the registers, but with only partial success. To increase the take-up, street *razzias,* as I have described earlier, were stepped up.

The years of occupation were hard, often frightening, sometimes exciting, and they demanded courage, purpose and tenacity. In these the Belgian people did not fail.

5

The Operation is Blown

ONE morning, very early, I received a telephone call from Antoinette de Ligne who, like myself, had stayed in the Motor Corps and with whom I was in close touch. She told me cryptically that 'visitors' had turned up at Rue Montoyer and that she would report for duty at the Corps. I understood at once: the home of her brother-in-law, Guillaume de Limburg-Stirum had been raided by the Gestapo. She was coming to see me – without informing any unseen listener to our conversation where we would meet. With great impatience and some trepidation I waited for her visit: how much did they know and who would be next on their list?

The morning wore on; I did not dare leave the house in Avenue Louise and kept twitching the curtains, looking for a sight of her familiar figure and ready to detect any unwanted follower, but there was no sign of her. Perhaps they had already visited her, too? By midday I could wait no longer. Security dictated that I should not ring her to enquire: if the Gestapo were in fact there, they would undoubtedly have the phone tapped and might be able to trace the origin of incoming calls. So there was still nothing for me to do but wait.

Nervous or not, I forced myself to finish off quite a lot of desk work which had been awaiting my attention, and then had to leave: that day I was down for duty at a canteen for debilitated children, in a Brussels suburb. Once there I could almost forget the underlying tension, but at intervals the same questions would surface in my mind: what was happening? Who would be next? Would they even be looking for me?

Eventually I went home, walking deliberately down the far side of the street and alert to any indication that things were wrong; but the house stood placidly there and all was apparently well. After a careful inspection I let myself in and indeed, all was still well, there at least. At 3 p.m.

I could wait no longer; I telephoned Antoinette's father, Prince Albert de Ligne, who was the head of the Belgian Red Cross. He was clearly irritated and disturbed that she hadn't turned up for lunch: she was normally punctilious in keeping him informed when her various duties kept her away from home. He told me that he knew nothing of his daughter's whereabouts, but he invited me to come and see him that afternoon. This I did, and we conversed briefly; I was at pains not to reveal that Antoinette and Guillaume were involved with the underground, knowledge which might well have been an embarrassment to him, in his position. Luckily, while we were talking Antoinette and her sister Bee arrived. They told us that, having entered the Limburg-Stirums' house that morning, by the back door, they were intercepted by a Gestapo agent who made them sit in the drawing-room while the house was being thoroughly searched.

They sat for a long time – hours, it seemed to them at the time – in semi-darkness; they could hardly open the curtains as closed curtains were a prearranged signal to Guillaume and his wife that they should not enter. In halting German the sisters tried to get some information from the Gestapo about the reason for the search, but their questions elicited no response. To pass the time, Bee (later Mrs Peter Whitwell), who was a good artist, vented her frustration by drawing cartoons of themselves, sitting beside each other on the couch, with chains and iron balls attached to their feet.

I immediately tried to find way of warning Guillaume. Eventually I managed to ring the house in the Ardennes where he and his wife were staying and was told that Guillaume had had a bad fall while out riding and was slightly concussed. Somehow he had to be got to a safe house; we had a job to do for the Motor Corps, not all that far from where he was, so we decided to go and fetch him the following morning.

In the meantime it was essential to give the 'stop' signal, which was always decided in advance, to the agents who were working with us, and also to warn Comte Jean d'Ursel about the course of events. I telephoned the d'Ursel address at Boitsfort but there was no answer. It was from this house that most of our Zero group messages were transmitted to London; Jean was, of course, one of the main organizers of our service. His house was large and stood in an extensive garden with several possible exits; this, we hoped, would make it relatively safe. Only the previous evening I had been there, taking with me a great deal of new information about the current state of several airfields. When approaching the house I had noticed a man in a grey raincoat, behaving

(as I thought) suspiciously. There was something about him which dis-
quieted me and I said to Jean and his wife, 'I think your house is being
watched.'

For a time we peered around the curtains in various directions but
there seemed to be nobody about. I was told, kindly enough, that I was
getting jumpy.

Now, I thought, if only I had put more conviction behind my hunch: if
only I had managed to convince them. My anxiety grew as I remembered that the d'Ursels had planned to be at home that day. Had the
Germans perhaps picked up several of our people? Could anyone have
talked? It didn't seem very likely: our agents were not in direct contact
with each other. To what extent was Service Zero itself blown? We did
not then know what we found out after the war: all the time there had
been a traitor among us.* I spent a restless evening, my mind imagining
possibilities. My family, it was plain, had noticed my nervousness,
though they could not have guessed the cause. At last I used the excuse
of a headache and went up to bed; I would need to be calm and in good
form the following day.

The next day was 8 October 1942; I got up early, went outside to a
public call box (safer than calling from home) and rang some of our
agents. It was then that my worst fears were realized: several of them
had been arrested.

Later I learned that Jean and Jeanne d'Ursel had been arrested and
taken to a prison in Germany. By then, Jeanne was three months preg-
nant and eventually she gave birth to a baby daughter, in a cell in a
prison in a north German town. While she was in labour there was an
Allied air-raid on the town and nobody came to help her. After the
birth, an exhausted Jeanne cradled the child to keep her alive and
warm, hardly daring to sleep in case she let go of the baby. Everything
possible was done through neutral countries, including the Vatican, to
have the child brought to Belgium – a baby could hardly be held
responsible for anti-German activities. And, in fact, after several
months of repeated requests, the little girl was returned through the
Red Cross; on paper hidden in her nappies, written in Jeanne's blood,
was the story of her birth. She is now happily married and lives in
Belgium with her husband and children. Sadly, Jeanne never came
back. In March 1945, only a month or so before the end of the war, she
was sent to the gas chamber in Ravensbrück. Jean returned to Belgium
after the war; though quite ill at the time, he recovered and became one

*In 1988 we still do not know who it was.

73

of his country's most distinguished ambassadors.

I now realized that there was nothing else for it: I must ask my mother to help. Throughout all my comings and goings on Resistance work I had always invented plausible reasons for my absences, knowing that it was better for her to know nothing of my other life. Should I eventually be arrested, it would be quite obvious to any intelligent interrogator that she was completely unaware of my activities and so she would be spared the worst kind of 'interrogation'.

I said, 'I need your help, badly. What I'm going to say will come as a surprise to you, and might even be dangerous for you to know. For a long time I have been working for the Resistance and now, as you must realize, things are starting to go wrong.'

'Of course I will help,' she replied. 'Just tell me all about it.'

So I told her about Madame Snauwaert; how she had been helping me by acting as a go-between for messages for the section in which I was working. Now I was afraid that the Gestapo were about to arrest her.

'Please go and ask her to destroy any messages she may have at this moment,' I said, 'and ask her to go and live with friends or relatives for the next few days. Just until the situation is clearer.'

My mother turned to me and said, 'Of course. I will go right away. Now I understand why you were away so often; I never did think it was all part of your work with the Motor Corps, you know.'

'I didn't want to involve you,' I replied. 'Papa is already a target for the Germans, and of course they know that Grandmother is English by birth and so they might intern her, if they want to be really nasty. I'm only sorry that you've been dragged into it now, but there's really no other way.'

'Now don't you worry,' she said. 'I'll put on my hat and go around there now. Whatever you do, take care of yourself.'

We parted affectionately; on my part I could only wonder what events the day might bring. Would I even sleep in my own room again that next night? Anyway, speculations of this kind were profitless; right now my first priority was to find Guillaume. Antoinette and I drove to the small village where the Limburg-Stirums were staying. We walked casually – at least, we hoped it seemed so – past their house, trying to detect anything suspicious, but all seemed quiet. We had evidently been seen by our friends for soon they came out and followed us to a nearby café. There we told them of the situation to date and its most serious implications.

Elisabeth was very calm and logical; I admired her greatly at that moment. She knew that even if everything went well, it meant separation from her husband until the end of the war; if it went badly, of course, things would be very serious indeed: KZ, privation, torture, death in any one of a dozen ways – a firing squad being the easiest option. There was a short discussion and a decision was made: we left Elisabeth to seek out some relations and took Guillaume to a safe house: the home of a greengrocer, who had long been warned to stand by for just such an emergency.

For several months Elisabeth lay low waiting to be useful. By the end of 1943 and the opening months of 1944, the Allied air-raids on Germany increased both in frequency and in intensity. Inevitably, more Allied airmen were shot down and found their way to one or other of the escape lines. They needed to be hidden, clothed and fed, and moved from one refuge to another. Elisabeth spoke perfect English and so was often asked to accompany British or American airmen on their journeys between safe houses. One such house was a brothel in Brussels and Elisabeth – the most unlikely lady to visit a brothel – often went there to collect a 'client'. On 3 April 1944 she rang the doorbell as usual, giving the accepted signal, but when the door opened she was challenged at gunpoint by two Gestapo men. Someone had talked – perhaps a German had infiltrated the escape line, masquerading as a Pole or a Czech. Elisabeth was arrested and sent to St Gilles prison in Brussels. There she spent five anxious and uncomfortable months, knowing little of events outside; in fact plans were being made to use whatever influence was available to procure her release. As the months dragged by, her friends and family were fearing more and more for her future.

On 31 August 1944 she detected a great deal of nervousness among the prison guards, mainly Germans. They were obviously transferring their archives and preparing for a move. Each prisoner was given a loaf of bread; it was officially announced that the prison was to be evacuated the following day. This was a bitter disappointment: the prisoners already knew, via the grapevine, that the Allied forces were getting close and already some prisoners were daring to anticipate freedom again. The next morning they were herded into trucks and taken to the Midi railway station in Brussels. Disappointment was tangible and relieved only slightly by the thought that the Germans were clearly engaged in their final retreat, back into the Fatherland. On the way to the station Elisabeth was able to slip a note through the tarpaulin cover of the truck, to tell her father, Prince Albert de Ligne, that she was being taken away. The note fell into the road, unnoticed by the German guards, but fortunately it was spotted and retrieved by a passer-by, who took it at once to her father.

At the station the prisoners were pushed into the usual cattle-trucks (forty men or eight horses), but so tightly that even at six o'clock in the morning the atmosphere was stiflingly hot. Eventually the train pulled out, its human freight trying their best to keep up each other's spirits; keeping up physically was easy enough – they were jammed together so tightly that it was not possible to fall, even if you fainted, as some people did. It was not unknown for such 'transports', as they were called, to arrive at their destination – Dachau or Auschwitz or wherever else – with the dead still jammed between the living. But at eleven o'clock the train stopped in a siding somewhere; there were loud voices outside then one voice calling loudly, *'Wo ist die Prinzessin?'** That was Elisabeth's maiden title and the voice was that of an SS officer. When Elisabeth responded, the door to her truck was slid open; she was roughly hauled out and told to follow the officer. As she walked the length of the long train she heard people within the trucks calling to each other: 'Poor lady; she is going to be shot.' Those at the tiny slits at each end of the coaches were passing back information to the people wedged tightly behind them. It was unnerving; she had, of course, no idea why she had been separated from her companions in misery. At length they reached the end of the platform and while the train slowly pulled away, the officer told Elisabeth that he was taking her to a Mr Nachtgard, where she would meet friends. This she found hard to believe as the name meant nothing to her. Together the two of them got into a car and were driven away.

Eventually the car stopped; the officer and Elisabeth went inside a house, her mind still in a whirl; this was evidently not another prison. To her amazement, she was handed a glass of champagne and invited to drink to 'better days'. Without her knowledge, it later transpired, it had been arranged that she should be exchanged for some forged papers and civilian clothes for the SS officer, who had obviously seen the writing on the wall. Soon she was driven back to a happy reunion with her family. Yet when her first joy had calmed somewhat she thought about her former companions in misery, by that time over the border and somewhere inside the Reich.

However, to come back to that fateful day in Brussels, in the autumn of 1942. Having lodged Guillaume at the safe house, I decided to return home, if it were still safe to do so. I walked past my grandparents' house

*'Where is the princess?'

76

that evening, apparently casually though with every instinct alert for the faintest indication that something was wrong, but there was nothing. Finally it was now or never; I let myself in and found my mother there, looking anxious. She told me that she had been to Madame Snauwaert's home, but had found the shop closed; this was, of course, most unusual on a working day. Luckily, however, the Germans had not left an agent there to trap any callers, as was their usual practice. My mother was looking around, wondering what to do, when a neighbour beckoned her over and said, 'It is terrible. The Gestapo have taken Madame Snauwaert away. Yesterday it was, and they have not returned. We fear for them.'

This news was a sad blow. I had, I thought, taken every precaution to shield her from suspicion, as she was a widow with a delicate daughter. I felt the responsibility weigh very heavily on me when we learned later that she had been taken to a KZ, but in fact she survived and was helped by my mother to get settled again when she returned after the war. During her absence we ensured that the daughter was well looked after; there were many such temporary orphans in Belgium in those sad days. In this case I later approached my great friend Geneviève Bracht to ask for help. She and her husband were kindness itself, and they saw that this little girl was well looked after. They also put their lovely apartment in the Grande Place at my disposal as a meeting place and provided me with extra food from their country estate.

There had been hardly time for me to take in the sad news when the doorbell rang. We were, of course, alarmed. A ring at the bell on that day could easily mean the very worst, but a quick peep through the curtains was reassuring: it was K1, Albert Kervyn. He looked harassed and told me that I was to leave the house at once and 'vanish': the Gestapo was expected at any moment. It was imperative to break the chain of arrests and I was 'blown'; for several months one of our people had been working at the Gestapo headquarters in the Avenue Louise and he had already been able to warn some agents in time for them to escape, but, sadly, not all.

(On the same day, my sister Bee, who was then at Jurbise, got a phone call from Madeleine d'Alcantara, to warn her that I was in danger. Unknown to me, so tight was the security, Madeleine was working in our organization. She was brave to try to warn me, but not so lucky as I was; she was later arrested and taken to Dachau, where she died early in 1945 – so tragically close to freedom.)

Having warned me, Albert wasted no time: there were other precautions to put in train. I prepared a small bag of personal necessities and went to the kitchen to pick up a few provisions. I did not want to tell my grandmother that I was about to leave her hospitable home but the dear lady evidently sensed that something was amiss. She entered the kitchen just as I was taking one of her *pains d'épice* (ginger-breads). I had to give a few explanations, say an affectionate farewell and then I was off.

It was with a heavy heart indeed that I left my home and family, not knowing whether I would ever see them again. All workers in the underground movement knew too well what they could expect if caught: dreadful interrogation and execution in some unpleasant and barbaric manner. To make matters worse, I knew that many of my friends in the service were already in the hands of the Gestapo; what would happen to them?

Our family cook, Marie Dury, took me into her own small apartment nearby when I told her that I was on the run from the Gestapo. Our cover story, for the benefit of anyone else who saw me coming and going, was that I was her niece, on a visit to Brussels; she called me Thérèse while I called her Tante Marie. One morning Albert came to see me. Clearly, something was very wrong: he looked white and strained, and my heart sank at the sight of him. We shared an inadequate breakfast – there was no chance of adding to the meagre official rations just then – and he told me that during the previous night he had avoided the German guards and got into Jean d'Ursel's house. Using a small torch he had located a certain hiding place in which were kept some highly compromising papers; these he had removed and burned. Poor Albert had been married only a week earlier and within a day or two both he and his wife Benedicte were arrested – what a honeymoon!

After a couple of days I decided that 'Tante Marie's' flat was becoming too dangerous for both of us; our cover story, by its very nature, could be valid only for a few days. So, reluctantly, I had to abandon this close link with the family; this time I found refuge with an old friend from the Motor Corps, Agnes Hendrickx. The house was very near Gestapo headquarters – so near, in fact, that I could see the comings and goings of the German cars which used the yard at the back of the house. That headquarters was later severely damaged in a daredevil daylight attack by a Belgian airman, Jean de Selys Longchamps. Knowing Brussels well, he flew at roof-top level along the main street opposite his target and attacked it head-on with cannons and rockets.* It was an

*The attack took place on 20 January 1943, and was carried out by two Typhoons of 609 Squadron, RAF. The two pilots were both Belgian: F/Lt Baron de Selys Longchamps and F/Lt André Blanco. Both machines returned safely.

78

amazing performance which not only, as I have said, caused a great deal of damage, but also raised the morale of many people in Belgium. Jean was a close friend of my family and we were very sad when he was killed in action later in the war.

At my new refuge Agnes was intelligent and lively, and she rather enjoyed the spice of risk and the sense of adventure involved in hiding me. She had been a wonderful friend when we were working together in France, in 1940, looking after the camps of Belgian army recruits. While I was there I even felt safe enough to make contact with some of our agents, discussing with them how they would keep the organization functioning once I had left for England – for that was now my intention and, in fact, the only course open to me. Nevertheless, as the war progressed the organization continued its work and the Hendrickx house was a refuge for many more people at one time or another.

My new identity card now proclaimed me to be Mlle Louise Bertier; among other cosmetic touches, my fair hair had now been dyed dark and so I was able to circulate freely. One day I was even able to meet my parents in a quiet allée off the Bois de la Cambre, in Brussels. It was an isolated place and we would have been able to spot anyone who might be following them. It was a sad goodbye: I knew I would be leaving for England as soon as the underground had made the arrangements, and the future was uncertain for all of us. I had, as I have said, never been able to tell them about my underground work; as a politician, my father would certainly have been watched by the Germans (and indeed, he was taken hostage during the following year). He told me now that he was sorry that I had not confided in him as he might have been able to help.

At this meeting I arranged with them the coded message which was later to be broadcast from England to inform my family that I had arrived safely: 'Louise has seen her aunt.' When it went out some weeks later it brought great joy to my parents and friends.

So now we parted, knowing that we should not all meet again until the nightmare of the war was over; we were in a public place, so demonstrations of affection had necessarily to be restrained, but it was a highly emotional moment.

Once I had gone into hiding, a man in civilian clothes called several times on my family, asking for me; failing to find me, he enquired about my possible return. Where was I at that moment? The same man called at Claude's house too: he was obviously in the service of the Germans. At both homes he claimed to have an urgent message from the underground movement. Whoever he was, he spoke perfect French with only the trace of an accent but his garb betrayed him: he wore a long, grey mackintosh – practically the trademark of Gestapo agents. My brother Francis, who opened the door to him, told me later, 'I could smell straight away that he was a member of the Gestapo.'

My family, of course, realized the danger – for themselves as well as for me. They contrived a story which they thought the enemy might swallow: I had eloped with a married man and the family wanted nothing more to do with me. The same story was told to anyone who called at Jurbise. Perhaps the enemy was convinced for before long the visits stopped.

By now the Germans were in possession of my cycle. Recently I had cycled to the Beauvechain region to check an airfield there: local reports were sufficient to suggest that some kind of interesting work was in progress. I was in a house, conferring with our local agent there, when a friend came in to warn us that several German cars had suddenly appeared in the village and at that moment a house-to-house check was in progress. We could not think what might have aroused German suspicions but clearly I must leave without being seen.

It was unsafe to go out by the front door and claim my cycle, leaning innocently against the wall in a narrow alley near the house, so I left by the back hedge and crossed several fields, as unobtrusively as possible, until I reached a main road. This was on a bus route and I made my way home, congratulating myself on getting away.

Eventually, however, the German searchers found the abandoned cycle and from its number-plate (all cycles were registered and carried such a plate) realized that the owner was not resident in the Jodoigne district. Eventually they came to the *maison communale** at Jurbise and asked for the name of the owner of the cycle. The clerk, who was no fool, realized that something was wrong and quickly altered the register; he gave them the name of someone who had died the previous year. Saved again!

After two weeks at the Hendrickx house I felt that it was not prudent to stay longer: life on the run meant changing lodgings constantly – any casual remark by a neighbour could be picked up in a shop or a queue by the wrong ears and then not only was the fugitive liable to arrest, but the innocent and kindly host family also. At the same time it was an odd feeling for me, to be cut off from my family and my home; but contacting friends was not too risky as the Germans would be unlikely to have a full dossier on my social life.

*the town-hall

The château at Jurbise, my home

Château de Vlamertinghe, where I was the day of the Dieppe landing

Author with her sister Bee and Eliane de Spoelberc meeting again in 1945

My parents, Comte and Comtesse de la Barre

My grandparents, the Marquis and Marquise du Parc

My brothers, (from left to right) Alain, John, Philippe, Francis and Xavier

Co-driver Princess Antoinette de
Ligne, 1945 *(Belga European Picture
Union)*

Waiting for patients at Tombeek

Our Motor Corps Unit

Author escorting Belgian Minister de Schriver, visiting Emergency Relief Camps
(Keystone Press Agency)

Mr Spaak greeting Princess Elizabeth of Luxembourg at the Emergency Relief
Camps *(Keystone Press Agency)*

German checkpoint in Brussels. *Razzias* became common *(Photographic Techniques Ltd)*

Belgians fleeing from the German advance, May 1940 *(Photographic Techniques Ltd)*

Training at the Emergency Relief Camps in Sussex *(Keystone Press Agency)*

Elegance went to their heads

Canteen at Anderlecht *(Centre de Recherches et d'Etudes Historiques de la Seconde Guerre Mondiale)*

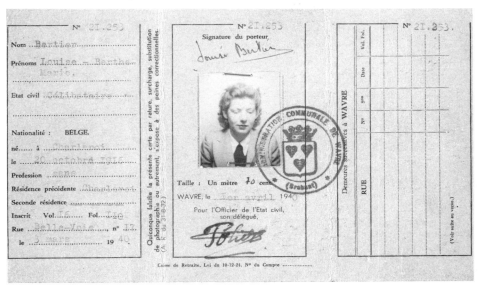

One of the identity cards used by the author

I was told to go and stay with Madame Royer, the head of an important Brussels hospital. She was a large and capable lady; I felt that she would be able to cope with any emergency. She was very much involved in acting as, or arranging, a base for those who, like myself, were in hiding and awaiting final orders to leave Belgium. She lived in a narrow-fronted, five-storey house, together with her elderly parents, delightful people with whom I spent many hours of happy conversation. Her son, whom we called the Dauphin, had lost an eye in battle in 1940. Despite this disability, however, he remained a talented cabinet-maker. His skills, no doubt, stood him in good stead when he constructed a false ceiling in the attic; this supplied a useful hiding place in case the house should be searched by the Germans.

Indeed, the enemy were still hard at work, trying to root out every member of Service Zero and other groups with which it might have co-operated. As time went by, we heard more and more depressing news.

On 7 October Jacques Pinte had gone to Florennes, to get more details about work going on at the airbase there. His instructions were to start with a reconnaissance at the nearby railway station, Warnant, so as to find out what materials were coming through for delivery to the airfield; then he should travel to the airfield and assess how the supplies were being used. It was expected that this mission would take several days, so Jacques got in touch with the local solicitor and house agent, saying he wanted to look around and see what land was available for purchase. This, then, would be his cover story.

He spent some time in Warnant station, trying to look like a would-be passenger, waiting for a train; in reality, he was watching various goods trains, counting the trucks and trying to assess what the loads were. After a while, in an effort not to be too conspicuous, he went into a café for a drink. Inside he was surrounded by four German soldiers and an NCO armed with machine pistols and was arrested. While in the lavatory earlier he had made notes on an eraser slate, so now he was able to put his hand into his pocket and wipe them off. He told the Germans that he was there to buy land and that they could check with the solicitor – which they did. All the same, he was bundled into a car at gunpoint and taken to the local *Kommandantur,* and from there to the prison at Namur. Finally, some days later, he reached the prison of St Gilles in Brussels and here he caught a glimpse of Albert returning from inter-rogation. This, he knew, meant that things were serious, but he hoped that his link with Albert was not yet established.

Jacques' house was then raided but his wife stood up to the Germans

81

in so dignified a way that they were heard to say, 'She must be the daughter of an officer.' In this they were correct: her father was a high-ranking French officer. Unfortunately, the Germans then found private letters, not connected with the underground but from Albert, thus proving beyond doubt the link between the two men.

Jacques, as it happened, spoke German perfectly. Indeed, he had once carried out an intelligence-gathering mission, dressed as a German officer and travelling on a German military train – with incriminating documents on his person! Now, however, while being interrogated he denied any knowledge of the German language; he was alarmed when he heard one of his interrogators say to another, 'Yesterday you told me that you were dealing with a spy network with one man called Kervyn and another called d'Ursel. I think I have another member of that group here.' After that the interrogation became much more severe and Jacques was placed in solitary confinement. All three men, Jacques, Albert and Jean d'Ursel, were sent to Germany a year later.

During one interrogation Jacques was told, 'We know that José de la Barre (my real maiden name) is your girlfriend and unless you co-operate with us, we will tell your wife.'

Jacques replied, 'Unfortunately, you are wrong. She is not, despite all my efforts.' This remark was duly recorded and after the war, when we had the chance to read captured documents, it gave great amusement to his wife, Solange, and to myself. Jacques was indeed, and remained, very happily married. At another time he was being interrogated when he noticed a map of a German airfield – annotated in his own handwriting. He could not imagine how the Germans had got hold of it. One of the Germans told the other that it must have been made by Pinte, but the other pointed out that Kervyn admitted having made it. Albert, knowing that things were going badly for his friend, had accepted the blame himself. When you consider what the Germans were capable of, that acceptance was an act of genuine heroism.

As if things were not already bad enough, Charles Woeste was now arrested: the stool-pigeon had done his work thoroughly. Charles had been with Claude when they realized that the house was surrounded by Germans; there was no other course open to them but to try to bluff things out. Charles, known to us as the 'Notaire', had got out of several tight corners before. This time, however, his luck was out: his captors were not impressed by his story. Claude, clutching papers which would have condemned us all, rushed past the Germans soldiers, temporarily off their guard, and ran at full speed after a passing tram, which he boarded. In the next street he transferred to another tram and so managed to escape. Only the previous day he had had a narrow escape from arrest: he was taking papers to Jacques' home when through the window he noticed the sleeve of a German uniform. Having arrested Jacques, the Germans had staked out his house.

Albert had been most unfortunate. After coming to warn me on 8 October, he then went to warn Charles, not knowing that Charles had already been arrested. On entering the house, Albert himself was arrested; later he was taken to St Gilles prison – a name of ill-omen for our group. At first the Germans acted comparatively mildly towards Albert, Jacques and Jean; there would be no serious trouble for them if they would reveal the names of other conspirators against the Third Reich. Such promises were always quite valueless and in any case it would have been unthinkable to have betrayed their friends. Faced with their inflexible determination to say nothing, the Germans increased the roughness of their interrogations, but despite intense pressure none of these three gave anything away, and neither did Charles Woeste. Jacques invented a string of false stories but each fell apart on being checked. They were all dreadfully tortured and were finally sent to prisons, first at Kaishan and then at Donauworth. In their final prison the men were allowed, to their considerable surprise, to meet and converse; this greatly helped their morale.

At Donauworth the German chaplain, Monsignor Gramman, was very understanding about the ordeal which they were suffering. One day they were all subjected to an extremely harsh interrogation, so cruel in fact that they doubted whether they would be able to endure the next session without breaking. The chaplain told them, 'Don't forget, your duty as Belgian officers is to say nothing.' He habitually gave great support and comfort to those about to be executed and was respected by all.

From this gaol people were taken before the *Volksgerichtshof,* the People's Court, headed by the infamous hanging judge, Roland Freisler;* from this court nobody ever returned – it acted merely as a rubber stamp on the death sentence. On the day that Jacques and Albert were summoned to attend, a note was brought into court. The judge read it, stood up and announced, 'Because of the situation on the Eastern Front, the Führer has ordered that all courts and similar bodies should immediately cease to operate and all available men should go to do essential work.' In this way and quite miraculously our friends

*Killed in his own courtroom by an air attack in 1945; by then courts were again functioning.

escaped what had seemed certain death.

Their occupation in prison was mending army boots, which the Germans apparently seldom bothered to collect after repair. The winter of 1944 was extremely cold and fuel was scarce; the prisoners found that the boots burned very well. By then, after several years of captivity, they were little more than skin and bone and so they felt the cold dreadfully. In the end, they had burned three thousand pairs of boots sent to them for repair; this was so large a quantity that it could not be overlooked and when a check revealed the massive deficiency, the Germans were furious. This, they said, amounted to sabotage of army equipment; my friends were sent to Dachau, tantamount to a death sentence. When they were eventually liberated by the Americans they were in a pitiful state – but at least alive. I still have a photograph of them leaving the KZ; they looked like walking skeletons, thinly covered with skin.

However, after this look into the future, back to 1942. Despite the ever-increasing danger of arrest – I could almost feel the net closing around me – and with many of my close collaborators and friends already in the grip of the Gestapo, I was still receiving orders about the running of the group and about the plans for our impending departure for a safer world. One cold, wet November day I was instructed to meet a contact in the Bois de la Cambre; when I approached the rendezvous, most cautiously as can be imagined, I recognized Robert Niewenhuys. I had no idea that he was working in the same section of the underground – a tribute to the high degree of security which we eventually achieved. It was a relief to hear from him that he and I and three others would be leaving the following day for England, after spending that night at Madame Royer's house. The other two, I found, were Guillaume and Claude, together with Albert Melot, who was to be our guide. That evening we hid carefully the few dollar bills and gold coins which we had been given: there was a risk of being caught and charged with currency offences – looked upon very seriously – yet we needed to be sure of some kind of convertible currency for emergencies. So Madame Royer baked the coins into the bread rolls which we would be taking to eat on our journey and the Dauphin carefully stuck a hundred-dollar bill on the bottom of my small, eye make-up box.

Early next morning we left, to start on a journey which we knew would be both arduous and dangerous – but with the hope of freedom at the end drawing us on. Our instructions were initially to go to Liège and there to board the train for Paris; on that first leg of the journey we travelled separately and ignored each other totally. As the train steamed southwards we looked out at the countryside which we knew so well; I speculated whether the others were wondering, as I was, whether we would ever see it again.

All went well and we caught the Paris train according to plan. The first real test was a demarcation line which the Germans had established somewhere between Liège and Paris. I had the bad luck to be subjected to a thorough and public body search. Robert, seated not very far away, looked on indifferently and in fact the money was not found and my forged identity card was totally acceptable. According to Belgian law, every citizen had to carry such a card and any German would start an enquiry by asking for it. But obtaining false identity cards was never a problem: in several towns we had friends who worked for the local authorities and so were able to issue a genuine card, testifying to a fictitious identity, whenever this became necessary. I had now become, as I have said, Louise Bertier; my card was apparently issued in the small town of Wavre, not far from Brussels, and bore the number of 21.253. I now had to be quite, quite certain that I had memorized and could repeat without hesitation or error all the details on the card (place of residence, date of birth and so on) and that I could even, if necessary, give a general description of the neighbourhood.

With this ordeal over, I sat back rather more confidently and by evening we were in Paris. It was cold and dark as the guide who met our train led us away from the railway station and it was very late when the five of us, each clutching a small suitcase containing a few essential items, arrived at a house in the Rue de Berry. Our guide knocked repeatedly but there was no answer. Had this operation also been blown? Had the French contacts decided that the risk was too great? Whatever the reason, it was unsettling. But the guide evidently had a reserve plan and we all set off again. It was pouring with rain as we walked through unfamiliar and blacked-out streets, with only one small torch between us, and our minds were beset by miserable speculations: what could have gone wrong? The guide told us that he was taking us to some reliable friends; there could be no question of going to a hotel as the Germans kept a close eye on all comings and goings there.

Eventually we reached a house in the Quai Malaquet where a charming lady gave us a friendly reception; our spirits rose. At once, makeshift sleeping arrangements were made for all of us: together with some of her grown-up children she organized a comfortable bed for me in the drawing-room, while in another room armchairs, camp-beds and sofas made an improvised dormitory for the men. By the time we retired we were all more than ready for sleep and I remember nothing until my eyes opened the following morning. Then our little party was split up; some went to stay at the homes of sympathizers while others went to get news of our further travel arrangements. Later on that day we met again to be briefed on what had been decided and then dispersed again to our separate refuges.

I spent that evening with the chairman of Wagon Lits, Baron Snoy, and his wife, and remained with them for some days. They were most helpful and kind, and I remember them with gratitude, but I remember also and very clearly how impatient I was to be off on the next stage of our journey. During those days of waiting the five of us met almost daily at a safe – we hoped – place, a different one each time. We had great discussions about the details of the next leg of our journey, its hazards and its opportunities.

I remember Claude telling us, 'When we get to the line between occupied and unoccupied France, we are bound to be chased by police dogs. I am taking some black pepper with me to put them off the scent. You ought all to do the same.' At the time, I remember, I was not convinced that this advice was realistic, so I did not take Claude's tip. Fortunately, as it turned out, he did exactly what he had advised us to do, and very useful that pepper turned out to be.

We had been lucky in our journeying so far and so it was easy to be imprudent; on several occasions I was taken to theatres or well-known restaurants, where we might have been recognized. In some of the better restaurants often used by German officers, food was easier to obtain; the rest of the time we were left with whatever our ration cards would supply, so that we were often hungry. Very little food was unrationed but as it happened one item that was both obtainable and unrationed was snails. I had never eaten them and regarded the idea with some horror, but hunger is a great inducement and finally, with some reluctance, I tried them. To my surprise, I became very fond of them – and still am, all these years later. Another time during our stay in Paris I went to see a play in which Yvonne Printemps and Pierre Fresnay were acting, and then on to listen to Sacha Guitry. I was dressed in an elegant fur coat belonging to Baronne Snoy and, what with my outfit and the civilized surroundings, wholly forgot that I was a wanted person with a false identity and ought, the conquerors thought, to be in a prison cell.

People dressed in great finery to go to the theatre. The ladies, perhaps to distract attention from their ageing dresses, wore large and eye-catching hats, decorated with flowers, lace and veils. Similarly, fashionable hats were to be seen at all times of the day in the streets; it might be thought that in 1942 elegance had gone to women's heads, in more than one sense. One evening we went on to a night-club called the 'Boeuf sur le toît'. The place was full of uniformed German officers and the floor show was clearly aimed at them: they were, after all, the big spenders. Charles Trenet would smile at them, and Jean Cocteau, accompanied by a beautiful young boy, seemed to be on the look out in that fantastic atmosphere for the material of a new play. How degenerate it all was! Fortunately, it was not the face of the real France.

During the ten days that we were marking time in Paris, we got to know that face: the face of the France of the Resistance. We met many people but, as at home and for the same reason, we never knew each other's names. Sometimes we met in a small, back-street office, or in a room in an insignificant house; we were offered coffee – a great luxury in those days – and we talked, comparing notes, but the names we exchanged were always assumed. There were times when I began to wonder who I really was!

Sometimes in the big house on the Quai Malaquet we would be visited by a willing and alert man whom we called the 'Little Man'. His real name was, I later found, the Abbé Labouge, and he was a leading force in the Resistance. He would appear suddenly, without prior warning, from an unobtrusive door concealed in the panelling, to hand over to us food vouchers, *tickets de ravitaillement,* and to answer – so far as he could – our anxious questions. He would invariably counsel us to be patient, then he would disappear again. Looking back I can only hope that, despite our personal obsessions, we were suitably grateful to him for his help and for the risks he was running on our behalf.

Eventually it was decided that three of the men would travel by train as far as the demarcation line; there they would leave the train and find a quiet place where they could slip across on foot. The line, we had heard, was not so closely guarded as, say, the Swiss frontier. The fourth man and I would remain for a short time. He would be given passes validating him as an employee of the Gardes des Voies et Communications – a branch of the railway system – and me as social worker for the same government department. We drew lots and it fell to Guillaume to remain with me.

The first three were to leave the following morning and Guillaume and I would follow a day later; we would all rendezvous, if things went according to plan, in unoccupied France. We watched our first team leave, with many heartfelt wishes for their success; we felt also anxiety for them, launching out once again into the unknown, and some fear at being left behind. Somehow, there had been strength in being part of so united a team. Once they had gone, Guillaume and I left our safe houses, just in case the others were caught and 'persuaded' to talk. We went to Montmartre to pray in the Basilica. As we left the church we noticed excited crowds around the newspaper sellers. Intrigued, we bought a paper: the headlines told us, 'To prevent a British invasion, Germany will now occupy the whole of France.' In fact, German forces had crossed the demarcation line, without advance notice, that very morning, 11 November 1942. The note from Hitler to the French government was handed over at 5.30 a.m. that same day, at least an hour after German forces had started moving in.

This, of course, put all our plans in jeopardy. How, we wondered, would it affect our 'advance guard' of three? And with the Germans now controlling the whole length of the Pyrenees, our escape route was in danger. We suppressed our fears: fear was a process of paying interest in advance on tomorrow's troubles and in any case achieved nothing useful. So that evening we dined in a bistro off our usual menu: soup, a dozen snails and an apple – all coupon-free – but the weather had now turned cold and wet, and it was difficult not to be disheartened. We spoke little and our thoughts were sombre.

The next day the Little Man gave us our passes; these would allow us to cross the border into southern France and we would leave by train that same day for Brive la Gaillarde, some miles east of Perigeux. What a relief: an end at last to waiting! We got into the train, still with some anxiety about a possible check at the demarcation line – even though that was now, in theory, non-existent. Would the Germans notice anything odd about my identity papers? Did I really *look* like a social worker for the Gardes des Voies et Communications? Would I be able to repeat, on demand, the particulars on my identity card? It was a new card, with a new identity, issued that very morning and I was trying desperately to remember all the salient facts about myself and details of all those other journeys which, according to the pass, I had already made.

In fact, all was plain sailing and we reached Brive without any bother. From there we took another train to Tulle, only a few miles away: here we hoped to meet Claude and Robert, together with Albert Melot, the link man on the escape route. Melot was then due to leave us and go back to pick up another such group. In fact, before long he was arrested and was lucky to survive the war and be able to return to Belgium. But our friends were not in Tulle. This was a great disappointment and the cause of much worry, until we were told that when crossing the demarcation line on foot, they had in fact been chased by Germans with guard dogs, as Claude had feared. They had had to run for their lives, abandoning what little luggage they had managed to bring thus far, but Claude used his pepper and it seemed to work: the dogs lost the scent and they were able to evade their pursuers. In their flight they had been diverted from their planned route and so were unable to reach Tulle; Guillaume and I, therefore, went on alone and it was to be several days before we met our friends again.

We were now able to make for Foix, in the foothills of the Pyrenees and just north of Andorra; on the way we spent a night in a sleazy hotel in Toulouse, where I was as much concerned about the possibility of being colonized by the local insect life as I was about being picked up by some local agent either of the Germans or of the Pétain government. The following morning we set off again and reached Foix without further incident. Here we were able to make contact with Madame de Seine who, we thought, might be able to give us information – either about our absent friends or about the next stage of our journey. But she knew nothing: all contact seemed to have been broken. We were advised to wait for twenty-four hours. That afternoon I went for a walk, enjoying the magnificent views of the mountains and trying to recover some serenity after the tension of the past few days. I must have succeeded, for I sat down in a field and fell asleep – and was roughly awakened to find a cow licking my face. This was a tremendous shock, of course, but appreciably better than being awoken by the Gestapo.

The following day we left Foix and were taken to a nearby village, where a local farmer was to be our guide. At last we had news of the other three: they had set out to cross the Pyrenees from somewhere in the same vicinity but their guide told them that there was too much snow in the mountain passes and he could not take them over. They had then left for the region around Pau, some miles to the west of us and not far from Lourdes; here the terrain was not so mountainous and they would try again, with another guide. I heard later that at Pau they had met Gerard Pinte, Jacques' brother, who was also a link in the escape route. Gerard had fortunately escaped capture when the Germans moved down through France, as far as the Pyrenees. He found a 'passeur', a guide who agreed to take them over the mountains from Arro to Biesla, in Spain. This, in fact, the guide did, but as they entered the village the

Spanish Guarda Civil arrested them and they were imprisoned in the local gaol. Spain did not look kindly on fugitives from Nazi-occupied territory, and all would-be escapers knew that once in Spain they must evade detection until they could get either to their own, or at least to a friendly, embassy.

From gaol Robert, whose father was Belgian Ambassador to the Vatican, insisted on sending a telegram to the Papal Nuncio, asking for his intervention. Once this telegram had been despatched, Robert adamantly refused to have his head shaved, an automatic requirement for all prisoners held in Spanish gaols. A grand churchman, he said, would not welcome somebody looking like a convict; this excuse was not accepted and he was duly shaven. In prison with them was a young man wearing Canadian uniform; when they talked of the Vatican being able to hasten their release this 'Canadian' listened with a half smile; he was in reality Jean Charles-Roux, who had taken part in the Dieppe raid and had managed to evade capture. His father was also a diplomat at the Vatican; later Jean Charles became a well-known figure in London, as a priest attached to St Ethelrida's church, in Ely Place.

Following the intervention of the Nuncio, Claude and Robert were released but at Bontagna, a little further on, they were re-arrested and once again the Nuncio secured their release. Eventually they reached Madrid and were fortunate not to be sent to the dreaded Miranda camp, where so many escapers spent a very uncomfortable time. Finally, the two of them reached Lisbon, whence they were flown to England; courage and determination (plus some influence in high places and a little luck) had paid off.

However, Guillaume and I, waiting to be taken across the mountains, knew nothing of all this. Our next instructions were to go first to Brassac and then to Merens. This was not an easy journey. We boarded the bus early one morning but the bus broke down; the cold was quite terrible but we thumbed a lift on a lorry, running on charcoal, which was already giving a lift to twelve people and itself gave the appearance of being on the point of complete collapse at any moment. We all huddled together until the end of the lorry's run, but we still had another ten miles to walk to reach L'Hospitalet. Strangers in this sparsely-settled frontier region were both conspicuous and suspicious, and every time a German vehicle passed us – which happened far too frequently – my heart beat faster. It is true that we both had convincing documents testifying to our identity, and equally convincing (we hoped) stories to account for our presence there, but even so ... Suddenly we turned a bend in the road and walked

90

into the arms of two French gendarmes who wanted to check our papers. While they did so, we started a polite conversation with them and I was relieved that my French education had left me with no trace of a Belgian accent – which would automatically have thrown suspicion on both our papers and our cover stores. Fortunately all went well; our papers were handed back to us and we went on. Eventually we arrived at L'Hospitalet, the last French village before crossing into the tiny and, nominally, independent republic of Andorra, lying in a kind of no man's land between France and Spain. From this point on, only our feet could take us over the high passes to freedom – our feet and our determination.

We had been told to contact the parish priest, who was known to be anti-German, so we headed for the presbytery. There we found Abbé Roo, a young and very likeable man; he agreed to help us but pointed out that there were difficulties. Only a few days earlier the Germans had combed the district and most of the regular guides had been arrested; thus our planned line of evacuation was disrupted. The original plan had to be rapidly revised; our new route would be hazardous, taking us over some of the highest mountains of the Central Pyrenees.

It was a daunting prospect but we had come too far to turn back and the thought of freedom was a powerful lure.

6

Over the Pyrenees and on to England

How could Guillaume and I manage to cross the Pyrenees in the middle of winter? Father Roo soon found a solution to our problem. He left us sitting, warm and comfortable, in his vestry, while he went to visit the village 'madame' on our behalf. He would, of course, know her by sight and by repute, but such a call was surely unprecedented? Yet this surprising co-operation of sin and piety produced effective action: a party of three smugglers had arranged to leave for Andorra early the following morning and Madame obtained their consent for us to accompany them. Hidden in the church, we waited for nightfall; through the windows we watched several groups of German soldiers and French gendarmes setting off for border control and we could only hope that the expertise of our guides would enable us to elude them. We had little to say but I suspect that Guillaume, like myself, was examining mentally every possibility which might confront us in the days ahead.

Just before midnight there was a knock on the door of the vestry; we opened it and there stood the priest and the three smugglers who were to be our guides and companions on what could only be an arduous trek over the mountains. We both inspected them carefully: sturdy men, clad in rough but serviceable clothing and each carrying a bulging rucksack. I thought that it was as well that they were our friends: they would be formidable enemies. They told us that we must leave at once, some hours ahead of schedule: the border guards had got wind of a planned expedition and we must get a start on them. We were not averse to this: with the tension which possessed our minds, sleep would have been impossible in any case. We had a silent supper during which, no doubt, they were as busily summing us up as we were them. On them Guillaume and I now depended; it would be no exaggeration to say that we were putting our lives into their hands. Up there in the mountains, in areas remote from any human settlement, we could easily be robbed and abandoned – if not worse – and in such a case our chances of survival would be slim indeed. Yet we must trust these fierce-looking strangers; there was no other course open to us. There was a discussion about what we should wear; our shoes were not suited to mountain trekking in winter. Finally one of them went out and was soon back again with two pairs of rope-soled espadrilles; if two pairs of socks were worn, they fitted reasonably well.

Then it was time. Very quietly we left the church with a blessing from Father Roo to speed us on our way. It was a cold, clear, crisp night; the stars sparkled brightly in a sky of intense blue, so dark that it was almost black. I could not help thinking of Christmas, only days away, and of all the good things normally associated with it; but in the Europe of 1942 the chant of 'peace on earth' was highly incongruous. War raged from North Cape to Biscay, from the Atlantic to the Caucasus, and we two insignificant fragments were risking our lives to travel a few inches across a map – but what a difference those few inches would make! It was the thought of that difference which sustained us now and gave us courage to face the days to come. We were going to need that courage.

Almost at once we had to cross the railway tracks, at a point barely sixty yards from a control post, so we went down on all fours and started to crawl. Then my rucksack became caught up in the signal wires beside the track and made them ring loudly in that total silence. One of the smugglers administered a dig in the side, quite roughly, as a warning that we could not afford that kind of mistake. At the noise we all froze and remained perfectly still; a light appeared in the window of the control post while, doubtlessly, sharp eyes scanned the track in each direction. But soon the light went out again; we breathed out in relief and even more stealthily resumed our journey.

Soon we began climbing and we climbed, it seemed, for hours. The smugglers were all fit men and accustomed to such exertions; they made their living by crossing frequently between France and Spain. We, however, had experienced the hardships of over two years of severe food rationing and so were by no means fit – even if we had been accustomed to prolonged exertion as severe as this. We found it extremely difficult to keep up with our guides, although the loads which they were carrying were far heavier than the few belongings to which we still clung. As the mountain slopes became steeper, we had to use our hands to prevent ourselves from slipping back, and these soon became bruised and cut; we had to summon up every last reserve of physical strength and tenacity of purpose to keep going. Needless to say, Guillaume and I had no surplus breath to compare notes, but it was plain to me that he was finding the going no easier than I was. Our hands, mercifully, became numb and our espadrilles were torn, but on we went, scrambling up impossible slopes, ignoring even the merciless cold. Whatever the effort, we never lost the realization that we were totally committed: there could be no turning back.

At about 3 a.m. we begged for a rest. Our sturdy companions, not in the least physically distressed by all their exertions, took pity on us and we sat down for a few minutes. We took the opportunity to eat a meal – of sorts: we opened tins of sardines and forced them into our parched throats, washing them down with a *coup de gnole*, a swig of harsh, locally manufactured spirit. The rest and the refreshment did us good and we resumed our journey; soon we were making our way through a snow-covered col at Envalira, 7000 feet up. By now it was full day and we would have found the scenery magnificent had we been minded to look around and enjoy it, but survival was the name of the game. At least, there was no fear of being detected, up here: in this desolate landscape we were the only living beings.

The sun came up and the temperature rose slightly, but over every rise there was another rise and we trudged or scrambled on with grim determination. By four in the afternoon we had reached an isolated house and here, we were told, we could rest for a while. The house belonged to a scattered hamlet and was at the end of a road – no more than a track – leading out of Andorra. Why there should be human habitation up here among the rocks I could not imagine but here it was, offering, we thought, shelter and a chance to rest. The residents showed no particular surprise at our arrival, no particular surprise at our spreading ourselves in their only living-room. Thrilled with sensuous delight, I threw myself on a bed but found at once that I was at such a pitch of nervous tension that sleep was impossible. As it turned out, this was just as well: within half an hour we were informed that an Andorran police patrol was near and getting nearer. It might be, of course, that we could buy ourselves off, yet this was by no means certain. We could well find ourselves taken back to France and handed over to the Gestapo: anything was preferable to that – even forgoing our desperately needed rest. The local people told us that as luck would have it a lorry was about to leave for Andorra la Vieja and we could lie in the back of it.

This was joy indeed; every turn of the wheels covered distance which else would have meant desperate physical effort. Guillaume and I risked the occasional peek out at the passing countryside, ignoring the lurching of our ill-sprung vehicle on the appalling track, rejoicing in the speed of our progress. Eventually, then, we came again to a town and here we climbed out; our magic carpet went no further.

Andorra is a freak of history: a small, independent state, sandwiched between France and Spain. It has two rulers: one the President of France and the other the Bishop of Seo de Urgel, who is Spanish. This complex arrangement, together with its isolated location, makes Andorra a haven for smugglers and, indeed, smuggling seemed to be the local industry, a way of life. We spent two days there in the capital while we negotiated for guides to take us on to Spain. Our other guides had exchanged salutations with us and departed, to pursue whatever shady deals had brought them thus far and to pick up a return load before turning back for France. Now we needed a new team, equally reliable, to take us on.

A stout man, who did not give us his name, offered to exchange our dollars for pesetas at what seemed to us, gullible as we were, a good rate; but the daughter of the house where we were staying pointed out that his 'pesetas' were worthless notes, issued by the former Spanish Republican government. We turned down the deal, whereupon the stout man became very nasty and hinted that he might well turn us over to the local police; this, again, would have meant eventual return to the Gestapo, the bogeyman of occupied Europe in those days. He did not, fortunately, carry out his threat; perhaps he anticipated unpleasant consequences for himself if he did turn us in. We wrote a letter to some friends in Spain; this had to be carried down and posted in Spain, for reasons of security, and the courier charged us 150 pesetas, a fortune at that time. We felt that we could trust nobody and became very anxious about our next move.

At last two Spaniards, Gonzales and Ribero, accepted our price and we decided to leave that same night; there was nothing to be gained by waiting and we were anxious to be away. Little did I realize that it would take us yet another seven days and nights to reach Barcelona. Our new guides were Republicans who had fought against Franco in the Civil War. The two men had been condemned to death by the Franco regime, they told us, having fought for the independence of their Catalonian homeland. In the aftermath of the defeat, both had been sentenced to death *in absentia*, and so could never again enter Spain legally.* Now

---

*Many years later an amnesty allowed all such exiles to return to Spain.

they made a living by smuggling contraband goods between France and Spain.

We started off at 9 p.m. the following day; our route lay initially along a narrow goat path hanging, it seemed, in mid-air halfway down a canyon. Fortunately, in the darkness we could not see the valley far below. It had been impressed on us that total silence was essential so we dutifully refrained from talking but were unable to prevent the occasional stone, dislodged by a foot, breaking loose and falling – audibly at first – into the blackness. Then our little column stopped quite suddenly and before Guillaume and I quite realized what was happening, we found ourselves staring into the barrels of two pistols, held by our guides.

Ribero said, coldly and dispassionately, 'Give us the money you are hiding or else ...'

It did not look good; how could we convince these desperadoes that we were quite penniless, apart from the money which we had to give them in return for their services? Somehow I found words to tell them the position and in my desperation I must have sounded convincing because the situation was suddenly less tense. I heard Guillaume make a rather poor joke; the muzzles of the two guns dropped and with a grin the Spaniards returned them to their holsters. Then they wanted us to shake hands in token that there was no ill feeling. Oddly, it might be thought, from that moment we were good friends.

They set the pace at one hour's walk and ten minutes' rest, but as the night wore on it became ever more difficult for us to get moving again after each pause. Accumulated fatigue and stiffening muscles were taking their toll; the cold and dry atmosphere at this high altitude, the rough terrain – often very steep indeed – over which we were moving, and the darkness, all combined to make progress difficult. At one time, I remember, we saw across the valley an entire village shining in the moonlight, while we were still in the shadow of the mountain. Numerous dogs over there began to bark; despite the distance, they must have sensed our presence.

Then quite suddenly the trail became even steeper: this was where we had to climb over the mountain chain at its highest point. I do not know what minister, prince or treaty fixed the Spanish border along the very pinnacle of those bleak and rugged peaks, but we certainly cursed the culprit that night. In later years I learned that the Pyrenees rise to 11,000 feet for much of their length. Looking back on our efforts, our suffering and our feelings of that night, I do not find the figure at all surprising.

Just before we reached the actual line of the frontier itself, we made a brief stop in an abandoned hut, evidently a well-known and frequently used staging post, which in summer would have been intended for shepherds bringing their animals up to the high pastures. Here Gonzales, whose French was more fluent than that of his colleague, gave us detailed orders for crossing the next, most dangerous, part of the mountain: total silence and special care in our movements so as not to dislodge any rocks. Even our precious walking sticks were taken from us. So we set off, tense and alert. Barely ten minutes later human forms were seen ahead of us and at a higher level; these were unmistakably the dreaded Guarda Civil and their silhouettes and tricorn hats were clear against the moonlit sky. We remained below them and in the dark, motionless, hoping not to be spotted for, although we were now in Spain, we were far from safe.

Ribero took out his revolver and I thought he might indeed fire at put my hand over his, to restrain him. Soon the high-mountain patrol disappeared over a crest; we gave them a little longer, for luck, and then started to move down the mountain as rapidly as possible. I was trying desperately to keep up with the Spaniards who were jumping from one rock to another, like mountain goats, despite the fact that each was carrying a heavy rucksack. After several hours of moving in what, initially, seemed to be complete blackness, our eyes became accustomed to the dark and we could see, after a fashion. In my concentration I could not even spare time to look behind to find out how Guillaume was faring but somehow he too managed to keep pace. When our guides thought that we had gone far enough for the moment, we stopped and lay on the unyielding rock, panting heavily. We were safe for the moment but now I realized that I had pulled a muscle in my right leg, and that from now on walking would become more and more difficult.

There are times in a woman's life when, even though the situation is crucial, feminine pride takes precedence over all other considerations. When we left L'Hospitalet I had stubbornly refused to part with a small bottle of Molyneux No. 5 eau de cologne and a tube of cold cream. The No. 5 was now used to massage my leg, Guillaume and the Spaniards taking turns as makeshift nurses. The cold cream came in handy for all of us, to ease faces and, especially, lips swollen by the extreme cold.

We now needed to find water. In our mad rush to avoid the Guarda Civil we had left the regular track and were now in *terra* comparatively *incognita* to our guards; but it was not until the coming of daylight that we found a spring of ice-cold water purling happily over its rocky bed, called a halt in a slight dip and sat down to prepare some kind of a meal.

We were now away from immediate danger; our surroundings were so stark and barren that we might almost have been on the moon. However, we did find some dead scrub not too far away, and we dared to make a small fire over which we prepared some soup from dehydrated broth cubes. Unfortunately, the cubes had been packed in a soap box and the consequent soup not only looked and smelled quite awful, but it also tasted strongly of soap. I was hungry enough to make an effort to get it down, and succeeded in swallowing most of my portion. Then the men produced from their packs pieces of lamb; these we cooked over the fire and ate with some bread. As dessert, one of the guides produced some almonds. At that time, in that place and under those circumstances, we felt as we would have done if, under normal circumstances, we had dined in a good restaurant. The rest and the food revived us all.

We spent the whole of that day zigzagging up and down the Spanish face of the Pyrenees. By the end of the day our clothes were torn and a gash on Guillaume's foot, sustained on a sharp rock, was becoming infected, so Gonzales and Ribero decided to take us to an isolated farm whose owners were friendly Republicans. In a single stone-walled room, miles from anywhere, we found a family with several children – they were in constant movement so that it was hardly possible to count them – cats, dogs, chickens and goats, all enjoying the warmth of a blazing fire and each other's proximity. One son seemed to be mentally deficient: he habitually moved about on all fours and whenever he came to rest, sat gazing steadily at us, mouth half-open. I, for one, found it disconcerting. At first it was difficult to make out the details of our surroundings: the room was filled with smoke from the fire and only as the smoke eddied this way and that were we able to see into this or that corner. Soon each of us was given a bowl of steaming milk and a huge ham omelette, and this meal thoroughly restored us. Relaxed now, I started to repair our torn clothes and the broken straps of our rucksacks, and the mother of the family put down whatever she had been doing to assist me in this.

But it could only be an interlude: we had to go on. Again we toiled up slope after slope reaching each summit only to be immediately confronted with yet another summit. We became so sick of feeling rocks always under our sore feet that when at last we came to the first road we had seen since leaving Andorra, we felt like jumping for joy. But our delighted anticipation was premature: any road in this area, so close to the frontier, was even more dangerous that the frontier itself, so we crossed it with great care and disappeared once again into the mountains. Before sunset we came to a completely isolated spot – so remote that once again we dared to build a fire. There was plenty of fuel for the gathering, so we laid in ample supplies to keep the fire going throughout the night and bedded down as close to it as we dared. We talked for many hours, or so it seemed, and tried to sleep, roasting on one side and freezing on the other. It was a long and uncomfortable night. When at last dawn came, in a typically Spanish outburst of excitement, our guides threw their berets into the air and fired at them, calling on us to join them in their brief moment of joy at being free.

For a few more hours we walked before we came to what had been intended as our first stopover: a primitive dwelling built snugly into the slope of the mountain. It was, we learned, a favourite port of call for smugglers generally. The family whose home this was seemed to be accustomed to the arrival of strangers unannounced and made us all welcome; we soon found out that they were sympathetic to the Republican cause, having lost a son in the Civil War. Two smugglers already there gave up their beds to Guillaume and myself, and we were touched by their generosity – a bed was high up on our list of priorities at that moment. The beds were constructed over a latticed floor, beneath which were the animals; the heat of the animals kept everyone warm and this constituted a very efficient, if rather odoriferous and primitive, form of central heating.

Before long five more Spaniards arrived, carrying bundles of prohibited merchandise; smuggling, they told us, was their regular occupation. They, like our two guides, were Republicans condemned by Franco even as we two were condemned by the Gestapo. They had heard of the Gestapo and this bond between us made for an easy-going relationship. We were all refugees, either from Nazism or from Franco, and soon we were sitting around the fire while they told us, as best they could, the story of their lives. When words became too hard to find and resentment too intense to restrain, a woman with a fine face and wearing a red scarf over her hair began singing revolutionary songs in a hoarse voice. We all joined in these emotive songs which I still remember. At the end we sang the Internationale; on that night nothing seemed more appropriate. It was not Communism that bound us all; it was not even politics of any recognized shade; it was just the expression of the deep and irrepressible thirst of humanity for a life of real freedom.

Gonzales and Ribero, Guillaume and I joined the other men for supper; following Spanish custom, the women of the family served us but did not sit down with the men. The meal consisted largely of meat as one of the sheep of the flock had been slaughtered for us. We drank Spanish wine, which was a great improvement on the *coup de gnole* of a previous meal although the process of drinking was both difficult and messy – for me, at least. The wine was in a pigskin container and the standard operating procedure was to raise the container above one's head, throw one's head back and direct a stream of wine into one's open and expectant mouth. My mouth was certainly both open and expectant, but vainly so: the wine hit my face from the hairline down and then, once I had 'corrected' my aim, soaked my clothing. Our hosts took pity on my inexplicable clumsiness and lent me the only *coppa* – cup – which the house possessed. This was a great improvement.

Despite the very primitive way in which they lived, these farmers seemed contented with their way of life. Their flocks were their wealth and from the sheep they derived most of the necessities of life. The grandmother sat happily all day immersed in the life of the family while her hands were incessantly occupied spinning the wool on a crude distaff. Meat was a major item of the family's diet. Their soap they made themselves of mutton fat mixed with very fine wood ash. The surrounding pine trees provided wood for the big open fire, on which all the cooking was done, and for the roughly hewn tables, benches and beds which were the only furniture. Only a few essentials, such as sugar and salt, had to be bought; an occasional trip to the nearest town took down wool and brought back a few necessities.

To give Guillaume's foot a chance to heal, we stayed two nights in this refuge; the family showed no sign of discomposure upon finding themselves so suddenly sheltering four unexpected lodgers and accepted us wholly as if we were relatives on a visit. I thought about them from time to time in the days ahead; was our citified life-style really superior?

And then we were again on our way, crossing the last peaks before descending to the Spanish plain. Now that we were fed and rested, and the going was appreciably easier, I had enough interest left over to look around me as we travelled. Even to us fugitives, our minds always outpacing our bodies in their eagerness to see over the next horizon, even to us the grandeur of the mountains was inescapable. At one point, and I can see it in my mind's eye even now, so many years later, we came over the shoulder of a ridge and there below us was a huge lake. It was a moment before I realized that below me was not water but a cloud sheet, filling a valley and contained by the steep and rocky mountainsides. Where we were, the sun was shining brightly; beneath that cloud, people were experiencing only a dull, damp day. It was several hours later that our trek brought us to the edge of the lake of cloud and we descended into it; in a few minutes we were soaked to the skin by its clammy wetness. Yet we were cheerful and did not regret our lost sunshine; we knew that by 10 p.m. or so we should reach a village where Republican sympathizers would take good care of us. As we descended in that grey light, there were olive trees around us and we walked slowly through them and down until we glimpsed the lights of the village twinkling for us. We were now far into Spain, near Lerida and about a hundred miles or so west of Barcelona. We almost felt safe, though we knew that we must still be careful not to come to the notice of the Spanish authorities.

Ribero and Gonzales now left us, with instructions that we should keep out of sight while they went to contact friends in the village; while they were gone Guillaume and I huddled together, trying to create some warmth against the damp chill. Our guides were gone much longer than we had expected and when they eventually returned it was with bad news: the Guarda Civil were occupying the village and it would be too risky to enter any of the houses there. But they had a hideout for us, a place where we would be safe. We followed them silently until we turned into a farmyard and entered a stable where there was a solitary mule. To our astonishment the animal was pushed to one side – a procedure to which he yielded only reluctantly – and Ribero uncovered a trapdoor hidden under the straw. He lifted the door and we descended a wooden ladder into an old, stone-vaulted cellar.

This, we were told, was to be our home for the next two days; the Spaniards got some clean straw for us – well, cleanish at any rate – and we all lay down, our teeth chattering as our cold, soaked clothes clung wetly to our bodies. We tried to light a fire but the resulting smoke made the atmosphere unbearable, so we lay down again and eventually managed to fall asleep. A squeak woke me up, and then another, and I felt something creeping over me. Alarmed, I woke the others; one of the Spaniards struck a match and set light to a torch of twisted straw and by its light we saw plainly – too plainly – dozens of rats running around. The men were angry with me for waking them up for so trivial a detail and I tried to stifle my anxiety. In this, fortunately, I was helped by my extreme exhaustion and eventually I even fell asleep again.

The following morning one of the women of the family brought us bread, meat and wine, an oil lamp and a few cooking implements. All this was most welcome. With hot water and a few rags I was able to give

101

rudimentary attention to Guillaume's feet, both of which were now in a pitiful condition. The loose stone, over which much of our path had led, had broken his toenails and the toes had become infected. I did the best I could to clean the wounds and to pull the remaining pieces of nail out of the flesh but the process was acutely painful. He bore it all wonderfully but his pale face and an occasional involuntary groan showed how much he was suffering.

Somehow our two days passed and it was time for us to leave; this coming stage of our journey would at least be easy – especially for Guillaume's poor feet – as our smugglers had arranged that we would be hidden in the bottom of a lorry which would take us to Barcelona. In the middle of the night we set out for the rendezvous with the lorry, which we reached in good time. Here we said goodbye to our Spanish friends. We were sorry to part with them as they had been kind and helpful after that first unpleasant experience at gunpoint. Throughout all our weary miles, every time I fell down from sheer fatigue they would always cover me with a blanket and allow me a few minutes' rest. They had always tried to help and now I wanted to show them how grateful I was. As a token I gave them my grandfather's gold watch, the only thing of value which I had with me. (As a footnote to this, many years later they wrote to me in England, asking me whether I would like to buy it back. I replied that I would, but I never heard any more.) As the sun rose they left us and headed back into the mountains; it was like parting from old friends.

Soon after this the lorry arrived and Guillaume and I lay down in the back while bundles were piled around and above us to hide us from view. For the next eleven hours we lay there while the truck twisted and turned on the mountain roads at what seemed to us a breakneck speed. At three separate places there were police controls; each time they moved one or two of the bundles in what proved to be only a cursory check – how they failed to hear the beating of our hearts I still do not know. That evening we arrived in Barcelona at last, tired and harassed, and were told that it was now safe to emerge.The driver indicated the whereabouts of the office of the British Consulate-General, so Guillaume and I set out in high hopes.

Unfortunately, although we managed to find the Consulate, by this time the office was closed for the day and the commissionaires on duty were most reluctant to open the gate for us. We tried to convey the urgency of our position and finally a man came out to us and offered to conduct us to a safe house where we would be hidden until the

Consulate could help us the following day. It was both curious and mildly discouraging to find that even in Spain, a sovereign and neutral state, it should still be necessary to use safe houses.

However, when we arrived we were greeted by a kindly-looking Spanish woman who seemed to welcome the chance to look after us. After the hardships of many days on the mountains, our cellar in the stable and the prolonged discomfort of lying on the unyielding floor of a badly-sprung lorry, it was wonderfully comfortable to be within a real house. I suddenly felt free, or very nearly so. But now that I could at last relax, a reaction set in. I felt ill and my teeth ached. It was soon found that I was running a high temperature; my toothache was, it transpired, caused by several abscesses; altogether I felt very poorly indeed – so much so that I remained confined to bed for almost a week.

When at last I felt well enough to return to the Consulate, to my joy the Consul-General himself took charge of me while Guillaume went on ahead. The diplomat in charge at that time was Harold Farquhar, who as an experienced officer had been selected for Barcelona, a key point in those troubled times. He and his beautiful wife were most kind and helpful. I had only the clothes in which I had crossed the mountains and by now, as will be imagined, they were in very poor condition; Mrs Farquhar presented me with many essential items and lent me some of her clothes – fortunately we were much of a size – so that I would look respectable during my stay in Barcelona. Several times I was invited to accompany her in the official car and on one occasion we went to visit the famous Benedictine monastery at Montserrat. After so long as a fugitive, even in her company I still felt very nervous every time I saw Spanish policemen, who seemed always to patrol in pairs. On such occasions I felt like dropping to my hands and knees in the bottom of the car and it took me quite a long time to realize that I was no longer being chased; that I could look any policeman in the eye and that here there was no Gestapo.

The usual route by which most fugitives of all kinds left Spain was via Gibraltar; getting there, however, was not easy, as there was always the chance of being picked up by the Spanish authorities and being confined in Miranda, a notorious detention camp. This might mean confinement at least until the end of the war and was a consummation devoutly not to be wished. To make things easier for me I was given a British passport in the name of Miss Barre; although this was a slightly irregular procedure, the fact that I had been born in England might well have helped. Next, I needed a cover story: I had, I was told, walked across the frontier on the

103

coastal road from Port Bou to Barcelona, at the south-eastern end of the Pyrenees, and somehow I had not seen the customs post – hence the lack of an entry stamp in my nice, new passport. On no account was I to say anything different. Another set of personalia to remember: this time, however, the process was easier as the details were largely correct. When my cover story was word-perfect I went with an official of the British Consulate to the Spanish Immigration Bureau; I told my story and noticed a Spanish eyebrow climb towards a hairline as the unlikely details were unfolded, but I could speak no Spanish and any questions were fielded by the British official. In the end my story was accepted, if not believed, my passport was stamped and I was in Spain of right.

One hurdle had been surmounted; now, however, I needed an exit visa, a *salida*, without which I could not cross a frontier outwards.

All refugees – Jews, ex-POWs, RAF, evaders, people like myself – all of us were anxious to get hold of a *salida*; we never knew when Franco might come to some kind of agreement with Hitler to send back any non-Spaniards in his territory; it might even happen that the Germans would march into Spain, *en route* for Gibraltar, and the whole ghastly nightmare would start again. We did not then realize that Franco was playing for time and standing up stubbornly to insistent German pressure. We did know, however, that Serano Suner, the Foreign Minister, was very pro-German and would have liked Spain to play a more positive part in German plans; hence our insecurity.

The day after my passport was stamped, I was placed on a train to Madrid, together with a clutch of other escapees; there we were housed in a small hotel and taken care of by the British Embassy, or one of its organizations. Here we were to stay until the necessary *salidas* could be arranged. I concentrated on passing my stay – my short stay, I hoped – in Madrid as pleasantly as possible. In the Prado museum I spent many hours among some of the world's finest paintings; it was a world far different from that of escapes, disguises and subterfuge and there I could even forget the strain of waiting for an exit visa.

In due course the *salida* came and in mid-January 1943, together with a group of Belgian underground workers who had just arrived, I left by train for Lisbon. There, to my great delight, I met Guillamue de Limburg-Stirum;* he was accompanied by Robert Niewenhuys and Claude de Villermont, who had been helped by the Papal Nuncio to leave Spain. I also found that my cousin, Serge d'Ursel, was there, as

*Guillaume came to England, joined the Belgian army and finally became an officer on the staff of SHAEF.

were several other people whom I had known before the war. They had managed to leave Belgium ahead of the German occupation and had got as far as Lisbon. Great was the rejoicing and in no time I was being wined and dined and generally well looked after. Indeed, I was even given some new clothes and I remember clearly the enormous pleasure they gave me.

I was enjoying myself so much, in fact, that I missed the first call for departure for England: I couldn't resist an invitation to spend that evening with friends at Sintra, some twenty miles away. We were never given advance warning when a party was about to leave, and it would just happen that a party was assembled and moved out on that one evening when I was out of town. Still, I consoled myself later, there would be many more chances.

While I waited I continued to enjoy the many pleasures of life in Lisbon. Portugal was, of course, neutral, and the city was full of Germans – many of them more or less camouflaged spies. We were briefed to be very careful what we said in public places – theatres and restaurants mainly. I enjoyed visiting the beautiful public buildings, but when I explored a little further I was horrified to find that young street urchins were often crammed together into one room, their only living quarters, and made a living by shining shoes or in any other way which promised money. Their families encouraged them to leave home; every mouth less to feed meant that the remaining children had that much more to eat. Fortunately, all of that is now changed.

On the evening of 2 March I was told that early the following morning I would be leaving on a flight for London. For security reasons, no more notice than that was given. (Even so a month later the Lisbon–London flight was intercepted by German fighters over the Bay of Biscay and shot down near the Brittany coast. All on board, including the actor Leslie Howard, were killed. Later it was said that the Germans believed that General Sikorsky, the leader of the Free Poles, was on board.) But finally I was on my way to England. As we neared the Bristol Channel all the windows were blacked out to avoid any possible spying, and not long after that we landed on an airfield near Bristol. What a long journey it had been and what a thrill to step out of the machine on to English soil – freedom at last!

7

Freedom, and the Work Continues

So at last I was free and in England; the goal of so much hardship had been attained. My feelings at having reached the end of so frightening and arduous a journey were too great to be fully described, but a huge weight, which I had been carrying for so long, had now fallen away. It was truly exhilarating.

From Bristol I left very quickly by train for London; the date was 3 March 1943 – it had taken me almost three months to complete a journey which nowadays we can do in almost the same number of hours. Now at last I could address my mind to a new, and happier, set of problems: what should I do next?

That last question was very quickly answered; the train pulled in to Paddington Station even as an air-raid was in progress. The first thing we all had to do was to take shelter. However, nothing much seemed to be happening so I managed to slip quietly away. I knew London fairly well but it was three or four years since my last visit. On top of that I had to contend with the blackout, and the noise of the anti-aircraft guns was unsettling. At 11 p.m., then, I set out to find the home of an elderly great-aunt who lived in Eaton Place.

Although I could find the right approximate direction, I soon lost my bearings; because of the air-raid there were, of course, no buses or taxis running, and I stopped a uniformed man to ask the way. In a strong American accent he offered to guide me, for which I was most grateful; he knew London very well and soon we reached Eaton Place. Here we parted; I expressed my thanks and he vanished into the gloom. I now found that my relations had very sensibly departed to live in the calmer atmosphere of Gloucestershire, leaving a couple to look after the house. Fortunately they recognized me; they suggested that because of the air-raid I should stay there that night, and they quickly organized a bed and a meal for me in their basement flat. Soon I was fast asleep, oblivious of the air-raid, and when I awoke the following morning it was to a typical London early spring day. I knew that I must find another sphere of activity as quickly as possible: I had been out of the struggle for too long. After breakfast, I expressed my thanks for the night's lodging and asked that my gratitude should be passed on to my aunt far away in Gloucestershire, and then set out for the Belgian Embassy to report my arrival. (I was rather annoyed, two weeks later, to receive a letter from my aunt; she pointed out that the next time I came to stay, I really should ask in advance! I decided not to burden her with the details of my prolonged journey from Belgium to England.)

The Embassy was, as it is now, in Belgrave Square; here the Ambassador, Baron Cartier de Marchiennes, made me very welcome and asked to be briefed on my adventures. When I had outlined the events of the past three months, he offered immediate help – as did Vicomte de Lantsheere, the brother of the commandant of our Motor Corps. There was also an invitation to stay with Renée Lippens and her brother, who lived in Dolphin Square; funds were provided to tide me over for everyday expenses until I was able to find a job and be independent.

Baron Cartier was an immensely popular and distinguished ambassador and was doing wonderful work for those Belgians living in England at that time. More than that, he had played a vital role in getting the Pierlot government to settle in London. Indeed, because of his friendship with Lord Halifax (then Secretary of State for Foreign Affairs) and because of his intelligent and astute presentation of telegrams received from the Belgian government, while resident in Vichy in 1940, he was able to strengthen greatly the position of our government *vis-à-vis* the British government during that crucial first year of the war.

Almost at once I started to meet many of the Belgians now living in London, most of whom were serving in one way or another. I was greatly struck by the contrast between their views and the views of our compatriots still in Belgium. Some rather considered that they alone were fighting the war; about the bravery, the danger and the sacrifice of so many very ordinary people at home, there was little knowledge. In the words of an authoritative study to be published some years later: 'There was always latent conflict between those who maintained resistance within occupied territory and those who, mostly for the best reasons,

107

worked from exile to maintain them.'*

There was much disagreement, also, among the Belgians themselves: some were very much in favour of the Pierlot government while others supported King Leopold in his decision to stay in Belgium and there see the war out among his people. I felt very strongly that this was no time for internecine struggle; here, as in other groups in a similar situation, a typical *emigré* mentality had come about. In my opinion a case could be made for both parties. Undoubtedly the King felt that he could best serve the nation by staying in Belgium, while the Pierlot government believed in keeping up the fight by representing their country in and from England.

Nevertheless, it was exciting to be in England, a free agent, and to find everyone immersed in the war effort. Among the British themselves I was conscious of a spirit of co-operation, of a shared national identity between all groups and classes. At first I had to attend several debriefing sessions: both British and Belgian intelligence wanted a very full rundown on conditions in Belgium and on the work of Service Zero – together with what little I knew of the work of other Resistance groups – and on our experiences while travelling. The British press also wanted to interview me; they seemed to be most interested in the details of life in Belgium under the German occupation. We had to take care, of course, not to reveal any information which could betray somebody still active over there; in order to avoid possible reprisals against my family, my real name was not used and I was called Mademoiselle B or Mademoiselle Suzette (a ridiculous name, I thought). There could be no full-face photograph of me but my hands were photographed; they, at least, could do nobody any harm. I particularly recall being interviewed by Barbara Wace of United Press; her article had wide coverage.** I had also, of course, arranged for the BBC to transmit the coded signal to inform my family that I had arrived safely: 'Louise has seen her aunt.' I knew that my parents would have been waiting anxiously to hear the message and I could well imagine the relief and the rejoicing. Relief and rejoicing, too, for those of my former colleagues still awaiting their turn to come out of occupied Belgium: the journey was indeed feasible.

In addition to the bare news of my arrival, I tried writing to my family; to do this I had to use a false name – which they would immediately see through – and use neutral channels. I also tried to send them parcels

---

Setting Europe Ablaze, Douglas Dodds-Parker (published Springwood, 1984), p. 72.
**This interview is given in full in Appendix A.

of food via Portugal and Switzerland; in addition, I did my best to ensure that my brother John, still in his POW camp, received Red Cross
food parcels via Switzerland. I was so pleased in 1944 to get a letter from
my mother, bearing a large blue censor's mark – *Geprüft* – saying 'My
dear Louise, so happy to get your news. We long to see you. Thank you
for the sardines which reached us last year. Don't send any more parcels
as we hope that you will soon bring delicious things yourself. Here there
are more and more robberies and murders. It is high time all this comes
to an end, but our spirits are high.' The letter was signed 'Monique'; the
'robberies and murders' referred to were the crimes committed by the
Rexistes, the neo-fascist party.

But to return to March 1943. I was uncertain what I should do and
while waiting for my ideas to clarify I started work in the American Red
Cross canteen in Charles Street. This was run by Margaret Biddle, the
wife of the US Ambassador in London, and although I enjoyed my few
weeks there, I wanted to do something more exciting than canteen
work. With the help of Audrey Sale-Barker (now Lady Selkirk) who
was a pilot in the Air Transport Auxiliary, I applied to join that organization. The idea of being a pilot was thrilling and when finally I was told
that I had been accepted for training, I was overjoyed. However, man
proposes but fate disposes: I was not destined to become a pilot. I was
told by Baron Cartier that I was needed to organize the Belgian
Emergency Relief: there was a dearth of suitable applicants for the job.
This, of course, was an order which I had to obey.

At this stage of the war considerable thought was already being given
to the problems which the Allies would face as they fought their way
across a disorganized Europe. There would be millions of refugees and
simultaneously a near-total collapse of all the services on which a civilized community depends: food, water, power, sanitation, medical care –
to name only some. The Emergency Relief Organization was set up to
follow closely behind the armies into newly liberated territory. One
thousand four hundred men and women of many Allied nations were
trained to deal with the problems which they would undoubtedly find. I
joined Mr Woolf, of the Red Cross, and Major Callens, an officer of the
Belgian army, who were organizing the section which would be responsible for Belgium and Luxembourg. Together we toured the country, visiting various centres where Belgian refugees had congregated,
and looking for suitable recruits. These journeys took us as far afield as
Cornwall, Wales and Scotland and there was no shortage of volunteers.
These all had to be screened for suitability but even so we were able to

109

find the men and women we needed. Recruitment was further boosted when the Princesses Marie Adelaide and Elizabeth of Luxembourg joined our organization, as did Madame Ganshof van der Mersh, the wife of the Belgian Solicitor-General, so that eventually our numbers were well up to strength.

There was still, however, an obstacle, if comparatively minor: even now, in wartime, the Belgian Ministry of the Interior demanded that we, the organizers, should all be reasonably fluent both in Flemish and in French. By then, of course, all of us understood English but the Flemish question was already an important political issue, so I had to take lessons every morning to polish up my rather basic Flemish. Our instructors in the organization were drawn from various sources; the British army took on the job of training us in operating field kitchens, cleansing stations and clothing depots, while social service experts prepared us for the wide range of other problems we expected to meet. We also learned how to run infant welfare clinics and first aid centres; after liberation it would be some time before all the normal organs of state would be in full operation. By the time D-Day arrived, in early June 1944, we were fully trained; from our camp in Sussex, not far from Haywards Heath, we watched the endless armada of bombers, fighters, transport planes and gliders streaming uninterruptedly overhead. This was what we had trained for and struggled for, and now it was all about to happen.

Some days later, it would have been about the middle of June, I was walking across a field near our camp, accompanied by a friend, when we heard the unmistakable noise of a V1 getting uncomfortably near. We knew only too well that at any moment that sputtering motor might cut out and the horrid thing would nose over and dive vertically to earth. Sure enough, not far from us the motor did stop and in the ensuing silence we threw ourselves to the ground and waited for the explosion. It came; the earth vibrated beneath us but we were intact. We got up again and found that the bomb had exploded in a field close by; the bloody remains of a cow testified plainly to what might have happened to us if the motor had stopped only a second or two later. What a mercy that the V1 weapon was delayed in its deployment, partly by technical problems and partly by Allied bombing of the launching sites. As it was, they were in every sense a headache. When one was approaching everybody felt peculiarly vulnerable but there was, at least, some kind of defence against the V1. Massed AA fire brought down several as they crossed the coastline; after that they could be destroyed by the new Meteor jet fighter, just coming into service, or by the Tempest. Under favourable

110

conditions, they could even be destroyed by the Spitfires – on one occasion, at least, by tipping the wing so that the beastly thing dived harmlessly into the ground. Against the V2, however, there could be no defence: it flew in the stratosphere and descended vertically at 3000 mph, outstripping its own sound. It gave, therefore, no warning of its coming: the explosion preceded the noise of its arrival. Fortunately, before too long the Allied forces had advanced so far that England was no longer within their operational range – which was, for both V1 and V2, some 300 miles at most.

My worst experience with a V1 was one Sunday morning in the summer of 1944 – 18 June; at the time I was living in Palmer Street, just behind the Guards' Chapel in Birdcage Walk. My friend Sylvia Duggan and I heard a V1 approaching; then the engine stopped and there was a momentary silence before a massive explosion which shook the building. So close was it, in fact, that some of the furniture moved and a window blew in, but fortunately neither of us was injured. I went outside to investigate and found myself looking at the ruins of the Guards' Chapel, where the emergency services were just starting to deal with the shocking numbers of dead and wounded. The Chapel had sustained a direct hit at a time when it was crammed with soldiers and civilians at a church service. That was probably the worst single V1 incident of all and a stroke of immense ill fortune.

The months between June and September, while the Battle of Normandy was taking place, were a very tense time. For us of the Belgian community the excitement was even more intense: the Allied armies were now so close to Belgium that our country must surely be liberated before very long – but when? We followed every development and pored over maps. The Americans, led by General Patton, broke through at Avranches and started to advance spectacularly to west and east. Paris was liberated; the British army raced across northern France and towards Belgium. Our hopes were high and our expectation at fever pitch, but despite all this excitement our training went on systematically, day by frustrating day; once our country was finally liberated, then we would be needed.

Then at last the 21st Army Group was racing through Belgium, so rapidly that there was little fighting and damage was slight. Antwerp fell. Thanks to the heroic co-operation of the Resistance, the Allied troops occupied the dock area before the retreating Germans could carry out their intended programme of massive destruction. The Guards' Armoured Division entered Brussels to an unbelievable demonstration of joy and gratitude. The excitement was helped by the supplies of champagne rescued from the Palais de Justice fire, but also by the very large stocks of spirits and wines that the Brigade of Guards had discovered in a warehouse just outside Brussels; this was the Wehrmacht's main supply for Western Europe. Some of this was offered in gratitude to Field Marshal Montgomery but he declined the gift: he was a teetotaller. Lord Carrington (later Foreign Secretary and Secretary-General of NATO) tied twenty cases of fine champagne to his tank – but when the tank crews sat down to celebrate, some time later, the heat and the movement had made it less enjoyable. War was ever wasteful! But the rejoicing in Brussels on that day of liberation was immense; after all, the emotions had been stored up for four years. If only I could have been there, up with the very first troops, to share the day! It was 3 September 1944: five years exactly since the British and French had declared war. Still, we listened avidly to the BBC and shared vicariously in the rejoicing – even finding some champagne of our own. The rejoicing went on for several days. Ghent was liberated, but the pace of the advance slackened momentarily and the victorious soldiers had a breathing spell in which to enjoy the celebrations.

It took the British time, and an effort, to get used to the kisses – not only from the women, which were acceptable enough, but even from the men, who thought their feelings on this occasion too great to be satisfied by mere handshakes! After all, they had waited impatiently – and had suffered – for over four years for that marvellous day.

Few people would be surprised to hear that after all our training, our courses and our exercises, it was now decided that our Emergency Relief had lost its purpose and that it should be taken over by the Ministry of Health. The Ministry was led by Dr Marteau, a colourful personality and a convinced Communist. I was asked to stay on but the work for which we had trained was not needed and I was not tempted by the prospect of a desk job.

Thanks to friendly contacts I had with officers working at SHAEF I managed to arrange an appointment as a second lieutenant in the Belgian army, attached to the American Delta Base in Marseilles. I very much enjoyed working with the Americans; they always got on with the job. If something had to be done, there was no hesitation about taking a car or travelling by plane to get quick results.

My function was to assist with the problem of Displaced Persons, a problem which was acquiring more and more importance as the Allied forces occupied ever more territory. So far as could be later calculated, there would be eventually somewhere between ten and twelve million people separated from their homes and even their homelands: ex-prisoners of war going west, mainly to Britain and France, or east to Russia and Poland; people liberated from KZs, concentration camps; slave labourers from the east trying to get back home; a few Jews who had somehow escaped extermination; later, German civilians who had fled from their bombed cities or from the advancing Soviet armies. Europe was in an indescribable turmoil; there has probably never before in history been chaos on such a scale. To sort out this immense confusion, to care for these people and help them to find their way back home – if there still was anywhere they could call 'home' – all this now became the responsibility of the victorious Allies. I knew it was going to be the kind of job which would make enormous demands on all those of us trying to sort things out.

The officers attached to Delta Base had also to deal with the large group of Red Army men – chiefly Ukrainians – who had joined the German army from prison camps. Hitler, who thought of Russians as 'chattels', agreed in 1944 that Russian prisoners could be formed into units under the command of German officers to bulk out the German forces, heavily depleted by the merciless battles on the Eastern front. The Russians had little choice: they could starve to death in their POW camps – and millions did – or they could go over to the enemy, with some hope of survival. Some Don Cossacks also formed a cavalry unit under the ex-Soviet General Vlassov. Many of these men were captured by the Allies or even gave themselves up, hoping to avoid being returned to Soviet custody. For the moment, they were held in camps.

I went to one such camp north of Marseilles, where the men were awaiting onward transport to Odessa; our job was to compile lists of names. I was struck by the awful sadness on their faces. They knew, even if we did not, what would happen to them once they set foot again in the USSR. But under an agreement signed at Yalta between Stalin, Roosevelt and Churchill, we had to return them; the boats which took them back would return with West Europeans who had found themselves caught up by the advancing Red Army. Some of these people had had dreadful experiences; many of the women had been repeatedly raped and were in poor condition. The G5 section of the US army was doing its best to sort out this deplorable situation and our work with these poor people was very rewarding.

There was a Soviet military mission attached to Delta Base and on some evenings we would all get together for a party. Inevitably, such gatherings would soon become rowdy; the Russians often became very drunk and then all the women present would be given lifts back to their quarters – a wise precaution.

At least one of the Wehrmacht-Russian units had shot its German officers before surrendering to a British unit and asking to be allowed to enrol in one of the Allied forces; knowing what awaited them in their 'homeland', they threatened to shoot themselves rather than be sent back. The British authorities on the spot quietly arranged for these Russians to join the French Foreign Legion and within days they were shipped out to North Africa. When this illicit affair became known to the Soviet government they threatened to retain all Allied ex-POWs under their control for an indefinite period unless the Yalta Agreement was rigidly upheld thenceforth. No other captured Russians escaped repatriation.

Before taking up my new post, I was allowed a short visit to Belgium, where I was reunited with most of my family. What a joy it was to be back on Belgian soil and to see so many dear faces again! It was an emotional meeting. I had a day at Jurbise with my elderly grandparents and even the arrival of a V1, exploding in the park and breaking several windows of the château, failed to diminish our joy and relief.* We had been lucky indeed: many families counted themselves far worse off now that the fighting was ending.

The reunion was brief, however; most of us were still involved in duties of one kind or another, and the time we could spare from more important matters was limited. My father was now Minister for Agriculture and so, as can be imagined, was particularly busy at this time. Bee was still working hard with the Motor Corps, a task which she had carried out unsparingly throughout the war – and indeed, would still be engaged upon for many months after the war had ended; it was quite a time before all the DPs in Belgium or of Belgian nationality elsewhere could be returned to their homes. Alain had joined the Allied forces as an interpreter, having served with the Armée Sécrète, and later stayed on as an officer in an artillery regiment. Xavier had also assisted the liberators with his knowledge of English; there was a shortage of maps, so people who knew the country well and who spoke English were especially useful. John was, of course, still a prisoner of war in Germany, though not for very much longer, we hoped; in fact it was the end of

*The Germans were now trying to deny the use of the port of Antwerp to the Allies – but their V1s and V2s were wildly inaccurate. Hence the craters at Jurbise, many miles from target!

May 1945 before he returned; his camp had been liberated by the Brigade of Guards but even then he had given first place in the aircraft bringing them home to those of his friends who had wives and children waiting for them. My mother was trying to reorganize the château after the appalling mess left by the last German troops before their hasty departure.

It was good to see my father and my mother both looking well, although thin; at the same time I was saddened by the news of members of the family or friends who were dead – many of them in KZs. A very favourite uncle, as I mentioned before, had been drowned while helping people to cross the Bidassoa into Spain: the current, swollen by heavy rain, had swept him away. Thus it was a happy time tinged with sadness, and all too short. Within a few brief days our family dispersed again as its members returned to their various duties.

We were all, needless to say, concerned over political developments in our country and had spent much time in discussion. By the end of September the Belgian government had been allowed to return from England with the duty of taking over day-by-day administration. The British, and indeed the government itself, for understandable reasons, had been concerned about the situation it would find on its return. What would be the attitude of the King? What would be the attitude of the armed Resistance groups? They had been in the thick of things, had endured years of oppression and hardship, had taken extreme risks and had paid a heavy toll in dead and missing – would they now demand an active part in running the country? The Allied High Command certainly did not want unrest; they were still busy fighting the war. Yet as things turned out, the return of the Pierlot government went off very smoothly.

The King, his wife and their children had been removed to Germany on 7 June 1944, perhaps for use as bargaining counters in the final days of the Third Reich. For a time there was deep anxiety about their whereabouts. With the royal family went my mother's brother, the Vicomte Gatien du Parc, who throughout the war had never left the royal children, in spite of the difficulties for his own wife and numerous children. Now we wondered about his welfare.*

One of the first acts of the newly-arrived government was to declare a Regency: the King's brother, Prince Charles, was appointed Regent. It was generally agreed that he fulfilled this function very well. Prime

*The royal family were liberated in Austria by the 7th US army, on 7 May 1945, and returned to Belgium.

115

Minister Pierlot and his cabinet had carefully prepared in advance a programme of measures designed to put the country back on its feet, and by and large these worked well. Certain financial edicts, for example the temporary blocking of all bank accounts, caused some transient disruption but were effective in protecting the Belgian currency against what might have been severe inflation.

I myself travelled from Jurbise to take up my duties at the US Delta Base in Marseilles. As I have explained, we were to have our hands full, trying to assist some of the millions of DPs as they were called. They had to be identified – not always an easy matter – and issued with some kind of document. During that frantic autumn of 1944 we were hard at work for many hours a day, screening and listing thousands of people, of every conceivable nationality, now housed in temporary camps. The screening was necessary not only to decide their future destinations – and some were now stateless – but also to comb out various war criminals and members of proscribed organizations such as the SS, who were trying to escape justice among the anonymous mass of refugees.

One batch of no fewer than 100,000 Italians were awaiting their return to Italy. I cannot clearly remember what their status was – some, no doubt, had been brought into Germany as forced labourers, while others had thrown in their lot with Mussolini when the Germans had freed him from captivity and set him at the head of a puppet government in northern Italy. Once we had documented them all as best we could, Major Callens and I were sent to Rome to arrange their return. The major had by then joined me as liaison officer at Delta Base.

On 11 April 1945, in Rome, we had the great privilege of being received in audience by Pope Pius XII, in his private study. I remember his very dark eyes and his impressive personality. Although by nature he was a very reserved man, he was of striking appearance and exercised an undoubted influence. In these days we would perhaps say of him that he had charisma. He spoke excellent French and appeared to be well briefed on our mission and its background. He came over not as a warm man but rather as a highly ecclesiastical diplomat. It was a long audience because the Pope asked many very relevant questions about the millions of DPs. For me there was one major problem: I was in uniform, with a tight skirt, and kneeling before His Holiness was not so easy; fortunately, however, protocol was not adhered to all that strictly in wartime, so kneeling was limited. The Pope gave each of us a white rosary and I treasure mine to this day.

Our audience was eminently satisfactory – quite different from the

116

one a few weeks previously when His Holiness had been persuaded to grant a mass audience to the press corps, soon after the liberation of Rome. On the appointed day a surging, elbowing mass of reporters and cameramen gathered in the audience chamber; a Vatican official tried to brief them on acceptable protocol while the men waited impatiently. When the Pope appeared the mob surged forward, cameras were raised, light bulbs flashed, shutters clacked and an irreverent voice loudly pleaded with him to 'look this way, Popey'. The Pope's welcoming smile froze on his face; officials moaned in horror and the rabble were persuaded to leave again as soon as possible. No Pope before had ever had to face such an ordeal and it is fairly certain that no future Pope will find himself in such a position. Undoubtedly, the lesson cut deep in papal circles.

Once we had made outline arrangements for the return of our Italians, we sped back to Marseilles to confront the next task. There was to be no shortage of work for many months to come. Slowly, very slowly indeed, comparative order began to emerge from the immediate post-war chaos.

I made many friends among the Americans and still correspond with some of them. Sometimes the base commander, General Rattray, would ask us to dinner. On one such occasion El Glaoui, the Moroccan leader, was present; he was a fascinating personality, very dark and with gleaming eyes. To his countrymen he was a great leader but the King of Morocco, perhaps fearing his enormous following in the country, had him removed in unexplained circumstances: one day El Glaoui just disappeared and was never seen again.

So 1944 drew to a close and speculation about the end of the war gradually died away: it was not going to be that year after all. That Christmas we were all startled, and for a time mildly concerned, by the Ardennes offensive – the last kick of the dying beast – but within days the sky cleared and overwhelming Anglo-American air power crushed the German advance and drove the survivors back into Germany. Yet it had been a frightening time, not only for the armed forces but for the civilians in the battle zone and immediately behind, facing the prospect of another German occupation. At least, as we later saw, Hitler had unknowingly speeded up his own final defeat: the tanks, guns, fuel and men lost in that last Ardennes offensive might well have slowed the Allied advance into Germany in 1945 – or at least, made the Anglo-Americans pay a much higher price for their conquest.

During the succeeding four months there could be no flicker of doubt;

117

early in May peace came again to a shattered Europe.

In August 1945 I was demobilized and returned to Belgium; the war which had absorbed all my efforts and thinking for so long was at last and incredibly over.

What now, I asked myself: what now?

8

What Now?

IN Belgium I rejoiced to be at home and with my family again, yet the insistent question remained: what was I going to do? The war had had, for me, two effects: it had removed, temporarily, long-term objectives while simultaneously broadening my horizons. My love for the family was the same as ever, but my attitude to life had changed. For a time, I thought, I would stay in Belgium, working for the Motor Corps when extra help was needed. This was not, of course, a long-term solution to my problem but sooner or later some other opening must present itself.

Almost at once I was given an opportunity to join my sister and Eliane de Spoelberch with a small convoy of ambulances to Czechoslovakia; we were to bring back Belgians who had been in concentration camps and who, in consequence, could travel only by ambulance and accompanied by doctors and nurses. When I returned from this very worthwhile venture, I spent my time either doing other such odd jobs which came along or helping to straighten out the château after the wrecking – fortunately, superficial – which it had sustained in the closing stages of the war.

It was a recurring joy, as the days passed, to see again so many old and valued friends, yet it was joy touched with sadness. So many people – good and brave people – had not survived. There were many celebratory meals where the conversation, inevitably, was of the 'do you remember the day when ... ' variety. On one such occasion I was asked to lunch with the Prince Regent; although he had necessarily to give many such parties, he himself did not enjoy them. His tastes ran more to small gatherings. This time he took part in the rather formal conversation dutifully enough but while his guests were later having their coffee, he whispered to me, 'Let's go and play ping-pong.' We slid unobtrusively

119

out of the room and settled down for a session of his favourite indoor amusement. He was an excellent player and no matter how hard I tried, I could never beat him.

As time went by I found that I was becoming more and more restless; my thoughts hunted around in circles, returning inevitably and constantly to the same question: what next? Slowly I formed a resolution to go to the United States; I had many friends there, most of them people I had served with during the last months of the war, and I admired their open friendliness and the direct way in which they went about things. What must their homeland be like? Yes, I would go to America; whether I would stay there or not, well, I would see. After a spell there I should be able to think more clearly about my future. When I made enquiries, however, it turned out that crossing the Atlantic wasn't all that easy: at that time, of course, there were no civilian airlines operating and there was still a shortage of shipping – and the position was made worse by the large numbers of service personnel returning home for demobilization. It was not until June 1946 that I managed to secure a passage in a merchant ship, a freighter, the MS *Stavelot*, sailing from Antwerp to New York.

Just before that time, while I was still in Belgium, I got a message from a friend in London asking me to see what I could do to help a friend of hers who had gone over to Brussels on business and had there been taken ill. Of course I agreed and went around to the Hotel Metropole; there I was confronted by a young man of extraordinary appearance. His face showed the colours of our national flag: yellow skin, a black eye and a red gash across his face. This was Charles Villiers, the man I was to marry some months later. He had been demobbed after serving with the Grenadier Guards and with the Special Forces in Yugoslavia, and had then resumed his career as a banker. This took him to Brussels, to renew business contacts; unfortunately, while there he had a bad attack of jaundice and was so ill he fainted in the bathroom, gashing his face and blacking an eye. My first reaction on seeing him was anything but romantic: what a sight, I thought. I knew that my family would be glad to look after him at Jurbise, where he would be less lonely and bored than in an impersonal hotel bedroom, so I drove him to my home where he stayed until he had recovered his health. We at once became good friends but neither of us had at that time plans to settle down; the unrest of the war was still powerfully with each of us. Eventually he departed for England and I sailed off to the USA.

As the boat pulled away from the quayside my family lined up to wave me off; my parents were resigned to the fact that it would be difficult to keep me in one place so soon after the end of the war. I waved back, knowing that I should miss them, but knowing also that I did not want to change my plans and stay at home. Then I went to look round the ship and prepare myself for the routine of the next few days. The *Stavelot* was one of the newest ships out of the Belgian shipyards; she had been ordered by the Germans during the war, but the shipyard workers ensured that she should not be finished while the Germans were occupying Belgium. The ship was designed with three propellers, for extra speed and manoeuvrability – the extra speed would assist her in fulfilling her intended purpose as a blockade-breaker, and her two sister ships, the *Bastogne* and the *Houffalize*, were similarly equipped.

As we slipped gently down the Schelde towards the open sea the evening sky slowly drained of light. We could not yet use any degree of the speed of which the ship was capable: even now, a year after the coming of peace, there were still occasional mines floating about. These represented a great hazard to shipping and until they could all be cleared, a very long and painstaking job, every sea voyage had the extra tingle of risk. Then, just after we had cleared Land's End, thick fog descended – surprisingly for that time of the year; the sinister noise of our foghorn evoked an occasional answering moan from the mist around us, and so the ship slowed and went cautiously on its way. At that time radar was not fitted to merchant vessels. Occasionally we would stop and a double blast on our siren would yield right of way to the other and unseen vessel. It was a strange feeling; in that main shipping lane we were surrounded by many other ships, small and large, yet they were all totally invisible. With the coming of radar, of course, such conditions ceased to present any real hazard.

Soon the fog lifted but now the sea became very rough. Nevertheless, the captain hosted his table for the first time since leaving port and we ten passengers – all the ship could carry – were happy to join him. That is, those of us who had not succumbed to the motion of the ship joined him. The captain was very experienced and wise in the ways of the sea; he kept us enthralled with accounts of ships he had sailed in; he described exotic places – Shanghai, Buenos Aires ... – in a way which reawoke the wanderlust in me. The dream of seeing such faraway places was, did I but know it, to come true in succeeding years. I was sometimes invited up on to the bridge and learned among other things that even in high summer icebergs are to be found astonishingly far south. At other times I was taken down steep ladders to the hold. All in all, my

121

first trip on a sea-going ship, as distinct from cross-channel ferries, was most agreeable and interesting.

At last, there was the famous skyline of New York. We moved slowly past the Statue of Liberty and took in the exciting view of all those sky-scrapers. Once on land, I used New York as my base and from there I explored the East Coast and even went up into Canada.

Then one day in New York the phone rang; the operator said it was a long-distance call – and indeed it was. To my surprise and joy it was Charles Villiers, with whom I had been corresponding. He came straight to the point: 'Will you marry me?' I was so taken aback that I could do nothing but stutter, so he told me, 'I shall ring again at this time tomor-row and confirm the offer.' Good bankers' practice, I thought. The fol-lowing day I said yes – and promised to take the first ship available and come back to Europe. By great good fortune I was able to secure a tiny cabin on the *Queen Mary*, which was still fitted out as a troopship. This time the Atlantic crossing was much faster than the journey out had been, but even so it was not fast enough for me. In Southampton, Charles was waiting. He planned to take all his demob leave, so far un-used, and set out on a tour of Africa; this would take several months. Could we therefore arrange to marry as speedily as possible and start on a protracted honeymoon?

This was easier said than done. My dear parents were rather conven-tional and if there was to be a wedding in the family, it was going to be a proper wedding. It would be an opportunity to throw off all the res-traints of the war years. We had to agree, of course, and a lovely celebration was arranged. I think, looking back, that after my long abs-ence the family wanted to show me off to friends and relatives and to many of my father's colleagues. In any case, Charles's grandfather had been British Ambassador to Belgium, and so his family had retained many Belgian friends. The wedding was to take place within the six weeks between our arrival at Jurbise and our intended departure for Africa: no mean feat of arrangement, considering how many people were involved. I must confess that I took little part in the arrangements as for a lot of the time I was travelling backwards and forwards to Eng-land, meeting various members of my new family.

In those days the Roman Catholic Church was much more narrow-minded about mixed marriages than it is today. The ceremony, there-fore, took place in the little chapel in the grounds of the château and the rites were cut to the minimum necessary to fulfil the requirements. Nevertheless, the Brabanconne and God Save the King replaced the hymns quite splendidly. Then we walked back to the house through the village where the schoolchildren were waiting their chance to wave the flags of our two countries and fireworks were let off with loud bangs. There followed a tremendous lunch, at which a roast sucking-pig seemed to take up most of the table, and the usual speeches; when it was at last all over, there was general agreement that it had been an exceptionally happy family day.

Two days later Charles and I left for Africa. Our intention was to find somewhere to settle down where we could carve out new careers for ourselves. Accordingly, we travelled from Kenya to Cape Town, and then up to Zaïre, driving an old Chevrolet delivery van which we had managed to buy cheaply. We had many adventures – contending with everything from poisonous snakes to the misery of malaria – yet we found that the beautiful places offered no promise of new beginnings, so eventually returned to England. Since then, life has been far from dull – but that is another story.

Appendix A

THIS is the text of an interview which I gave within days of arriving in England:

Since 1940 men, young and old, of every occupied country, have tried to get across Europe to reach a land of freedom. Women also have tried, and I am one of the lucky ones among them who have had the joy to get safely to England. I have just arrived after two and a half years under Nazi rule and every day I feel the joy of being free – but sometimes I am still astonished when I find that I can speak my mind without having to glance around me, without the fear of the Gestapo.

But in spite of the pleasure of being free and the extraordinarily good wartime conditions which I find here, I cannot help remembering my fellow countrymen still under the German oppressor and I would like to tell you a few words about them.

Hitler and Goebbels invented propaganda and naturally the free people of England fight shy of anything that resembles it. So do not think that it is merely propaganda when people from occupied countries state their case; do not think we are exaggerating or asking for pity.

No, we do not want you to be sorry for us; all we wish to do is to go on living, to be able to see the day when our countries will be free once again.

For two and a half years I helped to run a canteen for poor people in one of the poorest districts of Brussels. For two and a half years I saw every form of human misery pass through our hands. I saw little children getting thinner and thinner day by day and children by dozens being contaminated by tuberculosis – and when we did our very best to place them in a sanatorium to save these little lives, who had not yet had their chance, the answer nearly always was: 'We have not a free bed left.' The ravages are too great; we have not enough means in our power to help all.

In the canteen, I have seen daily hundreds of little children waiting in a row in order to receive their plateful of food. Can you imagine what it means to see those anxious and watchful eyes following us around, watching their neighbours, hoping to get just a little more than their share, then sitting down at their tables gobbling up the food, using their fingers more often than their forks in their hunger?

The tragedy of Oliver Twist was brought to me once again as I saw so many of these children come towards me with their empty plates, very often licked clean, and asking with begging eyes: 'Please give me some more.' It brought tears to my eyes more than once to have to refuse even vegetables, which were also so scarce.

Then I would move to another room, where we fed the old and weak; these were hardly more reasonable than the children. I remember a white-haired old gentleman, who stood waiting for hours by the kitchen doors, hoping to get scraps from the bottom of the saucepan; he was old, he was poor, he had not a penny to his name, but not so very long ago hushed audiences had applauded him when he conducted his orchestra in one of Belgium's most musical cities.

Others used to linger over their food, not because they were not hungry: on the contrary, they were ravenous, but as long as they were allowed to stay in the dining-room, they were able to enjoy the warmth of the room and so put off having to go back to their damp, dark and miserable homes. For there is very little coal; there is gas only at certain hours, and even electricity is rationed.

That flow of human misery was not only due to hunger, but also to the mental torture imposed on us by our Nazi 'protectors'. How can the Belgian people live normal lives when the ones they love are carried off to slavery daily? Men and women from all walks of life are suddenly seized upon by these slave-drivers and sent out to Germany in the most appalling physical and mental conditions. Young girls are torn from their parents and placed into camps before finally being made to work in some German factory. King Leopold and Cardinal Van Roey protested energetically against this, but Hitler's answer was to give the order that more workers must be squeezed out of Belgium; 500,000 workers out of a population of eight million have been press-ganged in that way. Furthermore, there are still 80,000 Belgian officers and men in Germany, in prison camps, and thousands of political prisoners filling German gaols. They are the men who have either worked for the underground movements of occupied Europe, or merely the innocent hostages who are satisfying Hitler's wrath. These men have tried to defend Belgium's liberty; they have given up their freedom and may yet give their lives for the Allied cause.

But do not think that if Belgium is downtrodden and weak for loss of blood, that she is discouraged; on the contrary; the morale of the country is still as strong as ever. We know that however weak we may be, we are still doing our duty and waiting with thumbs up for the day upon which we shall be able to greet our friends and allies.

In the meantime, Belgians of every class are doing their best against their oppressors. In factories, there is constant sabotage; many others do their work in underground movements, but I dare not for their sakes tell you much about them. Even schoolboys do their bit, stealing German bayonets and blocking up their cars with gravel in the engines. In every way possible, big or small, everyone tries to get a hit at them. A few weeks ago, the German *Oberfeldkommandantur* forbade smoking in trams, only because the gentlemen of the Wehrmacht had too often found that big holes had been burned in their field green uniforms. Never does one miss an opportunity to laugh at them and to make jokes about Hitler or the fat Goering. It makes them cross, and all those little things help one await the day of victory with less impatience.

The radio from London also brings great comfort to occupied territories and when the Germans talk of great victories in long speeches, and newspapers try to impress us with glowing headlines, the Belgian people just smile to themselves. They know the truth and the truth gives them courage, for thousands of them every night, behind barred doors and with no fear for the danger involved, listen to the voice of England and next day their friends and neighbours, who were prevented from hearing it, are told what the Germans try in vain to hide.

Another thing which gives – not confidence in victory (no one lacks that) – but greater courage, is to hear night by night the RAF roaring through to bomb German towns. Many Belgians lie awake and feel joy in their hearts, while their gaolers tremble.

Even in the daytime, occasionally, an RAF plane is spotted and often direct hits on German targets are commented on with eagerness, wherever our people gather.

I remember, not so long ago, being in a train in Belgium, when suddenly, with a creaking of wheels, it stopped and at the same moment we heard the buzz of a plane coming nearing. As one man, all the Germans rushed out and flew for nearby shelter. I suppose it was their guilty conscience which made them go so quickly, but on the contrary, nearly all the Belgians waved frantically to the RAF airmen, who, seeing so many civilians, waved back and passed on. In the joy, no one had thought that a bomb might drop, even when it came from an English plane.

Needless to say, this demonstration was severely punished and several people were arrested on the spot.

These little anecdotes will prove to you that the morale of the Belgian people is untouched. They certainly are very hungry and tired, but they know that the Allied Nations will one day bring back to them the joy and happiness of a free nation.

Appendix B

DURING the period in which Section 'Les Amis de Charles' was functioning, a large mass of detailed information was relayed to England. This information was concerned almost exclusively with enemy airfields: location; Luftwaffe units in occupation at any given time – types of aircraft and numbers; layout of each field with details of petrol and ammunition/bomb dumps; workshops; billets, etc. From time to time this intelligence would lead directly to an attack on a specific target; one such is detailed below (by courtesy of the Public Record Office).

On 29 August 1942, 13 B17E aircraft of 97 Bomber Group, USAAF, were briefed to attack the German Air Force 'drome at Courtrai/ Wevelghem. Over the target, one of the Fortresses found that part of the electrical system was faulty so that it was not able to drop its bombs. The remaining aircraft dropped 56,800 lbs of HE bombs in or near the target area; a further 2,000 lbs were dropped on the 'drome at Steene, near Ostend. During the course of the operation, three Fortresses sustained slight damage from flak (German AA fire) but no personnel were wounded or lost and all aircraft returned safely to base. One Me109 was shot down, while a further Me109 and one Fw190 were claimed as damaged, having broken off their attacks and turned away, emitting smoke. The American aircraft were escorted throughout the operation by four complete squadrons of RAF Spitfires.

Before taking-off the crews were shown large photographs taken by reconnaissance aircraft shortly before. On these were marked potential targets: fuel and bomb stores, workshops, aircraft shelters, heavy and light flak emplacements.

From later intelligence received and from pictures taken the following day by an RAF Photographic Reconnaissance Unit Spitfire, the damage caused by the raid was assessed as follows: 20 heavy bombs fell on the airfield and a further 2 on the perimeter track. One hangar, in use as a workshop, was seriously damaged. The ammunition store was hit. On the day following the attack, the wreckage of one Fw190 was still visible on the airfield. Casualties among GAF personnel could not be ascertained.

Appendix C

Administration of State Security

Department of Intelligence and Action

Network: ZERO

Section: Les Amis de Charles

CAMBRON

Born at   on
Resident
Was known to be in
Flossenburg in January 1945

DESMET, Georgette

Born at Velsique-
Ruddershove on 8.1.1918
Resident in Brussels
According to a letter from M.
Bertiau, she has now
recovered from an attack of
typhoid. Present whereabouts
unknown.

LADOS, Roger

Born at Schaerbeek,
19.8.1919
Resident in Woluwe St
Lambert

Was last seen in Flossenburg at the end of February 1945; he left there to work with a commando in the region of Linz (Austria), together with Messieurs Vanderburgh and Mertens, both of whom have since died.

MAINGOUX, Octave

Born   on
Resident
No news received

SELLECAERTS, Henri

Born at Schaerbeek on 21.1.1919
Resident in Schaerbeek
According to a letter in his own handwriting, he was then in hospital (23.6.1945) in Theresienstadt (Czechoslovakia).
He said that a move to an American hospital, either in Cobourg or in Gotha, was under consideration.

---

*Where there are gaps, information was never ascertained.

Appendix D

Administration of State Security

Department of Intelligence and Action

Network: ZERO

Section: Les Amis de Charles

LIST OF OUR AGENTS WHO DIED IN CAPTIVITY

(This list has been compiled from intelligence received to date, and may have been superseded by later news)

ALBERT, Henri
(Hon. Major)

Born in Brussels, 30.5.1882
Resident in Schaerbeek
Died in Dachau, 9.3.1945

d'ALCANTARA, Madeleine
(Countess)

Born in Ghent, 18.1.1917
Resident in Brussels
Died in Ravensbrück, about
13.2.1945

della FAILLE d'HUYSSE, Baudouin
(Baron)

Born in Brussels
Resident in Sottegem
Died in Belsen, 7.4.1945

de WOLFF de MOORSEL
(Baron)

Born in Brussels, 16.11.1891
Resident in Woluwe

Died in Flossenburg,
February or March 1945

DHOOGHE, François
(Hon. Major)

Born in Lièrre, 2.1.1881
Resident in Schaerbeek
Died in Kaisheim, 17.2.1945

GILSOUL, Robert

Born in Jodoigne, 17.7.1925
Resident in Jodoigne
Died in Flossenburg,
22.3.1945

HEYLIGERS, Louis

Born in St Gilles, 6.1.1878
Resident in Forest
Died in Flossenburg,
22.3.1945

LE JEUNE de SCHIERVEL
(Countess, wife of Jean d'Ursel)

Born in Pepinster, 28.10.1918
Resident in Boitsfort
Died in Ravensbrück,
4.3.1945

LEMPEREUR, Pierre
(Major)

Born in Liège, 27.5.1894
Resident in Brussels
Died in Flossenburg,
21.3.1945

d'HENDECOURT, Jacques
(Sgt)

Born at Ixelles, 19.1.1923
Resident in Brussels
Died in Flossenburg,
13.3.1945

d'HENDECOURT, François
(Sgt)

Born at Ixelles, 30.12.1923
Resident in Brussels
Died in Flossenburg,
27.2.1945

MERTENS, Henri

Born at Amsterdam
(Holland), 2.4.1918
Resident in Tirlemont
Died in Plattling, 2.5.1945

NEIRYNCK, Ernest

Born at Peteghem-Deynze,
1.12.1889

Resident at Ghent
Died in Dachau, 18.2.1945

PERSOONS, Hélène
(wife of Ferdinand Van Goethem)

Born at Molenbeek St Jean,
3.8.1889
Resident in Brussels
Died in Ravensbrück,
18.2.1945

ROUSSEAU, Victor

Born at Liège, 30.6.1904
Resident in Liège
Died in Flossenburg,
20.2.1945

SCHMITZ, Tom

Born at Anvers, 19.1.1908
Resident in Knocke
Died in Dachau, 3.3.1945

STIENLET, Paul

Born at Jodoigne, 29.6.1910
Resident at Jodoigne
Died in Dachau, 13.4.1945

TOBY, Rene

Born at Genck, 3.7.1922
Resident at Boitsfort
Died on transport from
Flossenburg to Belsen

VANDENBOSCH, François

Born in Brussels, 19.1.1900
Resident in Schaerbeek
Died in Flossenburg, 4.3.1945

van der BURGH, Yves
(Count)

Born at La Hayes (Holland),
6.1.1918
Resident in Ixelles
Died at Plattling, 2 or
3.3.1945

van ELDER, Jacques

Born at St Gilles, 19.4.1921
Resident in Ixelles
Died in Herzbrück, 5.3.1945

VERSPEYEN

Born
Resident in Solawe
Died in Flossenburg, 8.3.1945

Note: The recurrent names – Flossenburg, Dachau, Belsen,
Ravensbrück – are of course concentration camps. Plattling is on the
German–Czech frontier, south-east of Regensburg, and was probably
the site of a working party of KZ prisoners. Kaisheim is near
Donauwörth, and would also have been a working site, like Plattling.

Appendix E

Extracts from *Des Dossiers de la Police Allemande en Belgique*, Charles and Dasserois (L'Ecole Royale Militaire)

With reference to the espionage case 'Copine' (cf. the activity report of 3 September) a new enquiry has been set up under the title 'Jean d'Ursel'. The Belgian gendarme Georges Gillis, who had been previously arrested, has made a statement as a result of which twenty-one people have been arrested. Among them is the Belgian Count Jean d'Ursel, living in Brussels. A visit to his château, Jolimont, has led to the discovery of archives and documents, all of recent date, which furnish proof of the activity of a group working under the name 'Les Amis de Charles'. The Count d'Ursel is recognized as being the leading agent and the organizer of the group. He has admitted this but nevertheless he has refused to name his collaborators, who are mentioned in the confiscated documents only as cyphers: a letter followed by a figure in each case. It is clear that the group has drawn its support from the circles of the highest Belgian nobility and consists of people possessing the best military intelligence. Examination of the documents, running to several volumes, is continuing because of the results which they may yield.

According to those which have been scrutinized so far, the group possesses an illegal radio transmitter and also communicates with Paris and London by means of couriers. The overall chief is the Belgian Charles Woeste, and their activity is divided into various sections.

Organization
Special missions

Luftwaffe
Industrial espionage
Coastal region
Railways
General observation

Of the total numbers involved in this organization – more than 100 – thirty-four have been identified so far and twenty-one of these have been arrested. Further arrests may be expected as the enquiry continues. (4.10.1942)

In the espionage case 'Jean d'Ursel' (cf. the report dated 4 October) twelve further persons have been arrested. When arrested, the chief of the organization, Charles Woeste, was in possession of false identity documents in the name of Deprez. Further to this, the agent K1, Baron Albert Kervyn de Lettenhove, has also been arrested, together with three other agents. The enquiry has proved most difficult because all the people concerned are mentioned in the various documents only as cyphers. Nevertheless, some people have been identified and they are being interrogated.

In the course of the enquiry concerning Jean d'Ursel, it has been established that he created a network of accomplices who are all still at liberty and pursuing their activities by means which have not yet been determined. He was aided in his intelligence gathering by his father, Count Georges d'Ursel, and by his sister, Baroness Bénedicte Kervyn de Lettenhove, who have been arrested. Evidence reveals that the actual chief of the espionage network, Robert Niewenhuys (known as K18), used Jean d'Ursel to obtain intelligence on the results of the various missions. Nieuwenhuys is at present a fugitive. The enquiry continues. (4.2.1943)

In the espionage affair 'Jean d'Ursel' (cf. the report dated 4 February), the identities of eleven other people have now been established and six of them have been arrested. The others are being sought. One of those arrested, the telegraphist Jacques Dutoie, has confessed that he and his wife have been working since mid '42 gathering intelligence and passing it on to Baron Albert de Lettenhove. These missions were accomplished in Flanders and along the Dutch frontier, and consisted of ascertaining the strength, positions and movements of German forces. This activity dates back to a time previous to the

Dieppe operation. It is probable that some of those concerned belonged to another espionage group, led by Colonel Lentz. (4.3.1943)

With regard to the case of 'Jean d'Ursel', we have now succeeded in arresting eleven people, seven of whom are agents mentioned as cyphers in the organizational plan which has been captured. The agent known as G1015, among other designations, is now known to be the Belgian lawyer John Goormaghtigh, of Ghent, son of the professor of medicine Goormaghtigh. He has been led to confess that he supplied a weekly return concerning Wehrmacht use of Belgian railways. He was helped by ten collaborators and together they formed a section known as 'Railway Intelligence'. Valuable information about the Franco-Belgian frontier area, about most important military installations and defence works, have all passed through his hands. Other agents, now arrested, were known as T10, K7, H131, R18 and B6. It is certain that these agents have collated and passed on their intelligence. They have been confronted by the various proofs and confessions. A further ten agents will be arrested, having now been identified. The enquiry has been most difficult because of this use of cyphers to conceal identities. Large numbers of these agents have been living under false identities in Brussels and its suburbs. In the course of a search made at the home of Jean d'Ursel, the following articles were found:

One full can of automobile oil
One pistol, calibre '08, German army issue
30 rounds of ammunition.

(4.3.1943)

Bibliography

As I have said earlier, I have relied mainly on my memory and on certain papers which have been stored away since 1945. After so many years, however, memory has been less than adequate on certain matters and so for background information I have had recourse to certain authoritative books. For the help of any serious students of the period, they are listed here:

The Underground Press in Belgium (Belgian Ministry of Information, 1944)

Belgium Unvanquished, Roger Metz (Lindsay Drummond, 1942)

Facettes de la Vie et de la Guerre, Yvonne Dusser (Georges Thone, Liège, 1946)

The Undaunted, Ronald Seth (Philosophical Library of New York, 1956)

Message pour Pilomène, A.L.A.Beeken (Editions du Metro, Bruxelles, 1948)

Livre d'Or de la Résistance Belge, ed Leclerq (Bruxelles)

The Shadow War, Henri Michel (History Book Club, 1972)

Le Roi Leopold III de Belgique, Jean Stengens (Duculot, Paris Gemblout, 1980)

35, 1, 25, 30, 45, 8